THE POWER

of

TRANSFOCREATION

HOW TO CREATE, BE,
AND GET THE LIFE YOU WANT

FRANK FERGUSON

ISBN: 978-9968-03-244-5

www.thepoweroftransfocreation.com

Book Cover by Saheran Shoukat
Illustrations by Saheran Shoukat
01 Edition 2022

Disclaimer
The content of this book is for informational purposes only and is not intended to diagnose, treat, cure, or prevent any condition or disease. The information presented in this book is the author's opinion and does not constitute any health or medical advice. Please seek advice from your healthcare provider for your health concerns before taking healthcare advice from this book.

TABLE OF CONTENTS

Our Deepest Fear

By Marianne Williamson

Our deepest fear is not that we are inadequate.
Our deepest fear is that we are powerful beyond measure.
It is our light, not our darkness
That most frightens us.

We ask ourselves
Who am I to be brilliant, gorgeous, talented, fabulous?
Actually, who are you not to be?
You are a child of God.

Your playing small
Does not serve the world.
There's nothing enlightened about shrinking
So that other people won't feel insecure around you.

We are all meant to shine,
As children do.
We were born to make manifest
The glory of God that is within us.

It's not just in some of us;
It's in everyone.

And as we let our own light shine,
We unconsciously give other people permission to do the same.
As we're liberated from our own fear,
Our presence automatically liberates others.

Dedicated to my mom, Merna Simpson Kenton,
the warrior who inspires my life with her unconditional
and selfless Love.

INTRODUCTION

"The only limits in our life are those we impose on ourselves."
Bob Proctor

You may be asking yourself, what is the word *Transfocreation?* Or may I have misspelled the word *transformation?* No, I did not misspell it, even though I must admit that this book has been reviewed and all misspellings corrected by a better speller than me.

According to the Merriam-Webster Dictionary, transformation means "an act, process, or instance of transforming or being transformed."

Another source, Dictionary.com, defines *transformation* as *"the act or process of transforming, the state of being transformed."*

If you Google or search in a dictionary for the meaning of the word *Transfocreation,* don't be surprised to find out that the word is not there. Guess why? The simple answer is that the word did not exist before. *Transfocreation* is not only a new word but also a new concept. It's a new philosophy and a method that will help you create, transform, cure, develop, and improve your life in an easy, fast, free, and efficient way.

Transfocreation will help transform and improve the human race and the world. This concept can be applied to all people, the environment, and anything in the present and future.

Have you ever asked yourself how to lose that extra weight you carry around, how you can become spiritually, mentally, and physically healthier, how you can get the job you desire or start your own business, how to get that dream house, dream car, dream man/woman, how can you be financially free, be rich and have the money to provide for your family, how can you help to improve the lives of millions of people in need, and how can you save the environment from us, humans?

Let me tell you something; if you have ever asked yourself these questions, Congratulations! You have already gained 50% of your goals. You are already a winner! I can understand that you think. How can you achieve the success in life you always dream about?

By asking, *"how can I"* you create an infinite world of possibilities and begin to find a solution either consciously or unconsciously. The other 50% is recognizing your superpowers and learning to use them to *transfocreate.*

YOU ARE POWERFUL BEYOND IMAGINATION

You may be thinking, what the heck is this guy smoking? Is he on drugs? How can he see my present condition: My lacks, needs, wants, unfulfilled desires, and dreams? Let me answer this question. No, I'm not on drugs or smoking anything. I have in the past, many years ago, but it didn't give me the results I thought I would get.

But I can tell you that with the help of God and making a conscious decision to change, I could stop and open myself to a new me, i.e., a new version of myself that has attracted better things into my life.

Let's get back to business. Did you know that only 2% of people think, 3% of people think they think, and 95% would rather die than make an effort to think? It's a sad reality, but it's our world.

In 44 rounds of the earth circling the sun, I have seen, experienced, learned, and heard many things.

I don't need to see your present condition to understand what you are going through. I believe that whatever you are experiencing in the present will help you become what you were destined to be and that without a doubt is to be a happy, fascinating, fulfilled, and prosperous person!

You have infinite creative powers within you. You are capable of achieving more than you could ever imagine. You were designed and created for greatness. You have part of your creator's substance in your DNA; I'm not referring to your parents, even though you inherited their genes. I'm talking about the essence of what created everything in the universe. You were created in the *image* of God or the Creator, which means you can also manifest creation. You are a marvelous, powerful, and infinite unit of creation. You have everything you need inside to become anything you could have ever wanted!

Suppose more people like you *ask how* and not *why;* the world will be a better place because people will be *thinking* of solutions in the way you are presently doing by reading this book. The energy generated by their thoughts, good vibrations, and creativity will increase to such a high level that everything will be possible. People will be happier as they will achieve their desires.

When I told you before that you already have 50% of the job done, it's because just the fact that you ask yourself *how* and not *why* leads me to know that you are looking for a solution to your current situation. You are not grumpy and blaming everyone else or conditions for not being able to achieve what you wanted until now. Today is a new day; today, you will free yourself, and today you will *transfocreate*.

"If you must doubt something. Doubt your limits." Bob Proctor

---

CHAPTER 1

What are you?

Most people like to travel, especially when it's time to go on vacation. You could take an automobile, a motorcycle, a boat, a bus, or a plane to get to your favorite vacation spot. Since I love to fly, let's talk about an airplane. What is an aircraft? You might say it's what takes us in the air from point A to point B very fast. Or you could say it's something that flies in the sky. You could even say it's a big tube with wings.

No matter how you describe an airplane, even a five-year-old kid knows that an aircraft flies in the sky or is a flying machine. He might need help understanding the precise physics of how the airplane flies, floats, and soars, but he knows what an airplane is for: flying in the air above our heads.

What do you see when you look in the mirror? Of course, you see an image of your beautiful and marvelous self. But who really are you? You will not believe it if I tell you that as I write, I'm stunned and surprised that I had never asked myself or analyzed this idea when looking in the mirror. There is a first time for everything, I guess.

We all have different ideas of what we are: A man, woman, boy, girl, name, profession, skill, or function. Nothing I just described could ever represent and express a complete person; this is where the problem begins. What am I? What am I here for? Most people don't know what or who they are, why they were created for, and what they are here to do. We see the function of everything that exists or we have made, like airplanes, but when we look at ourselves, most people don't know what they are or why they are here while living in this plane of existence.

THE HUMAN BRAIN

The brain is the most sophisticated, incredible, and less understood body part. The human brain is what separates us from other species. The reason is straightforward; we can think and reason. Science, philosophy, theology - and many other branches of knowledge - have tried to describe and understand the human mind. They are making significant advancements, but the more they discover, the more they realize that there is much more to learn about the human brain's capacity, capabilities, and functions.

WHAT ARE YOU?

You are a spiritual being with intellect that lives in a body. We are all spiritual beings. I'm not a scientist, theologian, or philosopher since my background or formal education is in engineering and business, but I can tell you that from what I have read, studied, researched, and perceived, per my intuition, that as humans, we are *creative centers.*

We were designed to create, and our mission and everything we do in this life should be focused on creation. It's sad that no one ever told us this during childhood; maybe no one has told them either. Imagine what your life would have been, knowing from the get-go what you are and your purpose based on your design and functionality. I'm pretty sure it would have made things easier.

The good thing is that it's never too late, and as one of my favorite rappers said,

"And if you don't know, now you know, nigg@"
The Notorious B.I.G

CREATION AND FUNCTIONALITY

A bird was created to fly, a fish to swim, a dog to protect and be our best friend, a cat to be a cat and say meow, a flower to display the beauty and a sweat essence, a fruit tree to produce fruits and feed us, the sun to shine and give us light and warm, and a cloud to provide us with rain and shelter from the sun.

A chair was created to sit at, a table to eat or have a good conversation, a car to drive us around, a pen to write, a book like this one you are reading to remind you of what you already knew, a basketball to make three-pointers like Stephen Curry or become the best basketball player or our generation like Lebron James.

Everything was created for a definite function based on the need to satisfy or express something. The only creature on this earth designed with the highest capabilities of the universe needs to learn and understand his role and why he was created. Funny.

By being conscious and aware of our design and functionality, we live a different life in which every want, desire, and wish will be fulfilled by tapping into our original design and functionality to be *creators*.

DREAMS, CREATIVITY IN ACTION

We are all amazed and mesmerized by the performances and creative genius of great athletes, singers, actors, artists, designers, painters, musicians, scientists, philosophers, and writers. We tend to think of them as something incredible and supreme. We usually imagine them as superhumans with superpowers.

We must understand that the only difference between them and us is their ability to transform images of their thoughts and desires into the materialization of a final product. We can explain this: they are terrific dreamers and creators of dreams.

When we internalize this concept or idea and see ourselves as **creative centers,** we will begin to tap into a new reality - a new world of infinite possibilities. A new life will emerge from our inner DNA, a part of us designed for a reason and purpose. You will start to look at life from a different perspective, stop competing, and begin to create and collaborate.

Imagine living in a world where we are all *creative units*, interconnected and consciously using our capabilities to work together to create new things and ideas. We can thus transform existing ideas and things into new ones and collaborate on teams to solve the most daring and life-threatening problems such as sickness, diseases, poverty, hunger, global warming, climate change, pollution, and others. For sure, this will be amazing. I genuinely believe it's possible, and it's our only way out of the current messy situation we are living in.

My intention is not to point a finger and play the blame game toward any institution, system, or government since they can't and will not change until the creative units running these entities are aware of their perfect creative nature and decide to work as a unit for the benefit of humanity. We were all designed with the same substance and purpose, living in the same place - planet earth.

You are a *creative center.* Your ability to create and transform any circumstance is inside you. Creative powers are in your DNA, programmed by the original substance used to make you. All you need to do is access that creative and formless substance with your spirit through your thoughts. Doing so will allow you to materialize anything you truly desire.

IMAGINATION: THE CREATIVE POWER

"Imagination is more important than knowledge," Albert Einstein

Merriam-Webster dictionary defines imagination as *the act or power of forming a mental image* of something *not present to the senses or never before wholly perceived in reality.*

Let's look at the meaning of knowledge from the same source: *The fact or condition of knowing something with familiarity gained through experience or association.*

Since one of the brightest minds the world has ever seen gave us a hint into the secret of creation, we should always keep this quote by Albert Einstein fresh in our minds. When I first read it, I was struck and amazed. At the moment, my understanding of imagination was limited to my current consciousness, awareness, and paradigms. My knowledge has expanded now that I have a better consciousness, attention, and shift in my paradigms. This might not be your experience, but let me translate the quote more understandably.

Whatever you can see or visualize in the form of a picture or movie in your mind is what you will be able to create or bring into the physical world. This could be something tangible, a concept, a feeling, or an emotion. That supreme ability you have of *"imagination"* is by far more important than all the books, education, money, or anything in this world. Why is that, you might be asking yourself? Everything that was is and will be created starts with an idea in the *imagination.* If you can imagine something, you can and will make it.

You are a powerful, marvelous, and unique creature. You are a divine creative center. Think, imagine, and create the life and reality you want! Do what you were designed to do.

—

CHAPTER 2

User Manual

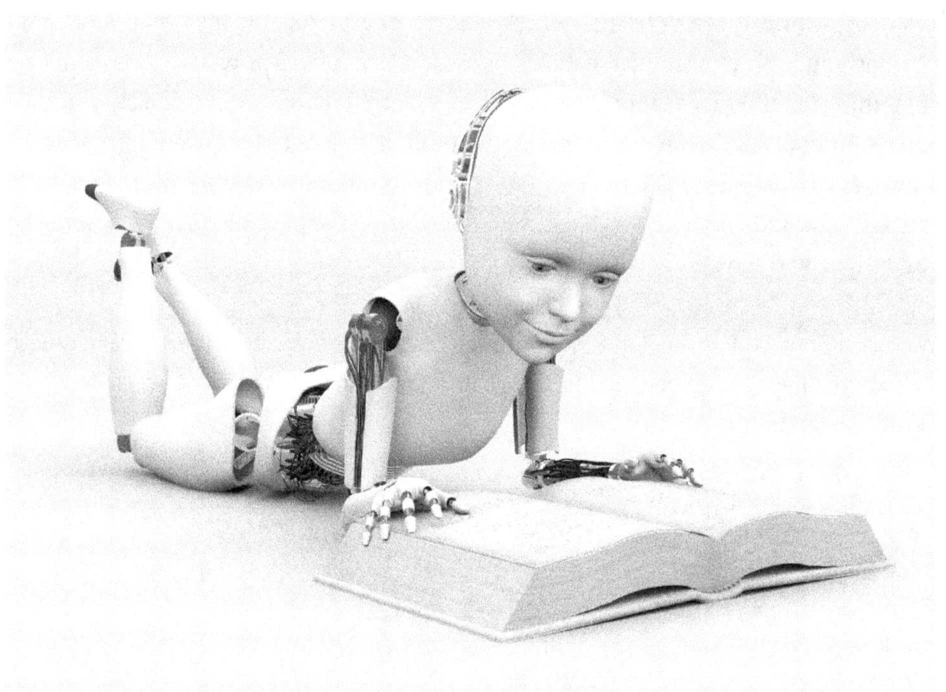

Your washing machine, computer, automobile, and telephone have two things in common. One, it was created by someone, and second, the creator provided a user manual for you to know how they function. It's essential and recommended that you read and understand their specific manuals before you use the abovementioned things.

You read the manual to gain basic knowledge of the use, capacity, limits, and maintenance you must provide. You also read the manual because you want to know the different functions and benefits you will get by operating these things in the best possible way, according to their manufacturer.

We are the most sophisticated, forward-thinking, superior, and incredible *creation* on earth, or creative centers, as I said in chapter one. *Why* don't we come with a user manual from our creator that tells us how we function and operate ourselves to our highest capacity?

I'm pretty sure that if we have such a user manual in our possession and we read, understand, and use it, we will consciously do and achieve amazing things! As a creative center, you can think, be, do, and achieve anything you can imagine. You are the most sophisticated, intelligent, and capable creation on this planet.

Once you understand the materials or substance used to create you, the purpose of your creation, the different functions of yourself, and the powers you were granted, your life will never be the same. You will tap into a new, magnificent dimension of awareness and consciousness and see possibilities everywhere.

To understand how you function, let's first analyze the moment before your creation, your design's reasoning and purpose, and the prototype and materials used. Also, let's look at the attributes, qualities, and powers your creator embedded in you when *He* thought of creating you during creation.

OUR CREATOR

> *"And God said, let us make man in our image, after our likeness: and let them have dominion over the fish of the sea, and over the fowl of the air, and over the cattle, and over all the earth, and over every creeping thing that creepeth upon the earth."* Genesis 1:26(KJV)

When the creator decided to create man, he modeled his creation after himself. By image, we understand *His* physical form and attributes. God can be manifested in many forms since he is a formless substance with the power to become anything in time and space. Our creator is an infinite intelligence capable of creating just by thought and word; He is beyond time since time is in Him.

Listen to this paragraph written by Wallace Wattles in his book, *The Science of Getting Rich.*

"There is a thinking stuff from which all things are made and which, in its original state, permeates, penetrates, and fills the interspaces of the universe. A thought in this substance, Produces the thing that is imaged by the thought" (Wattles, 2015).

Before our creation, the world was created and established. The sun, moon, stars, skies, oceans, animals, plants, and trees were created. Our creator decided to make us for us to use, administer, manage, and dominate the entire creation.

Our creator decided to make us in his *image and likeness*, which means that we look, function, and have some of his characteristics and essence. To do so, God used or gave us part of his substance or DNA so we could look and act like him. This statement is impossible to prove with the scientific method since we will need to have God in a lab, subtract a sample of his blood or substance, and then do DNA sequence testing. But there are other ways to prove it by using our imagination and sense of deduction and observation.

If you are a father, mother, son, or daughter, you will share a physical likeness with other family members. Also, you can notice nonvisible traits such as character, personality, taste, abilities, and intellect. All these before-mentioned similitudes are possible and evident because we share the same substance: blood and DNA.

As creative centers, the highest and most advanced creation ever achieved and produced is another human being or a new life. Before my daughter was born, I was in awe of the entire process from conception. I felt a powerful electric energy flow out of my body that traveled to fertilize the egg in the uterus of my daughter's mom. That physical, creative moment was something I would never forget since I was fully aware of the moment and time of conception. I knew that I was creating a new life at that precise moment.

By the way, I even told my then-wife that she was pregnant at the precise time. She did not believe me, but the technology proved otherwise thirty days later through a pregnancy test. She was 100% pregnant. That experience helped me understand our infinite creative powers and our true nature.

Thinking now about that magnificent creative moment before my daughter was born, when my mind was entirely in tune, and I wanted to procreate, I wanted to have a child and was thinking about it. That makes me understand that our creative powers are beyond the physical self. Conscious or subconscious, everything is created first in our minds with a thought. Then our bodies execute actions that lead to the results we think and imagine.

We are made of the substance of our creator. If you go back to the paragraph by Wallace Watters, it talks about a *thinking stuff and a substance* from which all things are created by *"God."* Humans are thinking units, just to put it mechanically or functioning way. We have the utmost ability, one that no other species in this world has: the ability and capacity to think. If you look around right now, you see the book you are reading, the audio you are listening to, the video you are watching, your car, and your house. Someone thought about it and decided to materialize his ideas into valuable things.

Now that you understand who you are, you will begin to see things in a different light, which will lead to a magnificent and more meaningful life full of possibilities within.

THOUGHTS AND WORRIES

In 2005, the National Science Foundation published an article summarizing research on human thought per day. It was found that an average person has about 12,000 to 50,000 thoughts a day. Of those thousands of thoughts, 80% were negative, and 95% were the same repetitive thoughts as the day before (National Science Foundation, 2005).

There was another exciting study (Leahy 2005, Study of Cornell University) in which scientists found that 85% of what we worry about never happens. With the 15% of the worries that did happen, 79% of the subjects discovered that either they could handle the difficulty better than expected or that the problem taught them a lesson worth learning (Leahy et al., 2005)

The conclusion is that 97% of our worries are baseless and the result of an unfounded pessimistic perception. These groundless worries are a significant source of stress and tension; they cause exhaustion for the mind and the physical body.

Imagine going forward after knowing that only 3% of your worries are authentic and could affect you, but 97% are baseless. Would you continue worrying about everything? I'm pretty sure you would not.

Before the study conducted at Cornell University in 2005, one of the greatest artists of our time (Bob Marley) released a song named, *Three Little Birds*. In 1977, he knew something about the nature of worry.

> *"Don't worry about a thing 'Cause every little thing is gonna be all right."*
> Bob Marley and the Wailers

Reparadigming Your Mind

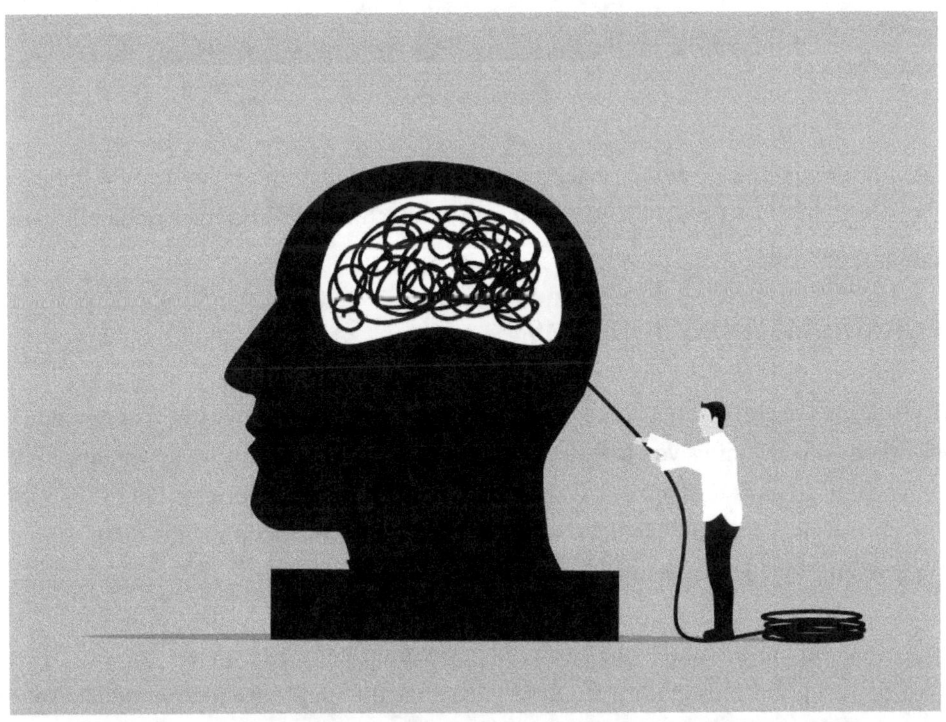

Reparadigming or reprograming your mind is the goal you should develop to successfully *Transfocreate* yourself, your environment, and any circumstances or situations life has and will offer you.

When stating "life has and will offer you," it implies that you must take whatever life offers. At one point, you must view circumstances, situations, and events as offerings and not as something you must or have to take, accept and agree to. You have the power and right to control what and when something can or will affect you, no matter what your situation is or will be.

For example, imagine that you are in the middle of a stormy rain pouring all over; you are soaking wet and cold. It will be so for you if you think you are dry and hot in the Sahara Desert.

Don't let yourself or others make you think about being dishonest or fooling yourself into thinking this way when it comes to having desires, aspirations, ambitions, and dreams to improve your life and allow you to become the person you were created to manifest - which is a magnificent, opulent, and beautiful reflection of your inner self.

> *"Anything the mind can conceive and believe, it will achieve."*
> Napoleon Hill

Do not let yourself or others make you believe what they think you should believe. Remember that you are the director, scriptwriter, star actor, and cameraman in your movie, your life.

PARADIGMS AND PROGRAMS

Paradigms are programs that control everything you do or don't do. While you are sleeping and dreaming, you are unconscious in a sense. Then you wake up conscious. Maybe you go back to sleep and wake up again. Such programming works 24/7/365; it never stops controlling and executing every thought and action while determining your results and achievements.

We can compare paradigms to a computer program because they are invisible, just like the program or software running your smartphone, computer, or tablet. Your mobile phone can download applications, make video calls, receive emails, play games, transfer money internationally, and buy products online. Have you ever thought about how a small object can do so many things? I'm sure you do. Do you know that the program on your mobile phone is more powerful and capable than the supercomputer used to execute the mission that landed the first man on the moon in 1969?

Programs or software are robust. Everything in the universe is run by a program or type of software that dictates motives, actions, purpose, and desired results. You must understand that truth to appreciate, learn and dominate the power you have to transfocreate.

So are you and me. We could be running on someone's program, doing and getting the results we don't want or like in life and not knowing why. This is not entirely our fault since we did not create our program.

Is that not scary to you? Of course, it is. But it will no longer be the case after you finish reading this book; you will have learned how to create your success-proof program, starting from where you are and with whatever you have now. You will have learned the *Art of Transfocreation.*

You might be asking yourself, how is this possible? Am I a computer running on a program? Well, yes, sort of; we all are. You are the most advanced computer that was ever created and will ever be created on planet earth. Your processor or brain has the capacity and power to generate significant quantities of electricity; that is just one of the lesser features of the vast catalog of capabilities the brain possesses. Your past, present, and future results will depend upon the program running your conscious and subconscious mind.

AMAZING FACTS ABOUT THE HUMAN BRAIN

"On average, a brain weighs three-pound or 1,400 grams of mass. That material controls every single thing you will ever do. From enabling you to think, learn, create, and feel emotions to controlling every blink, breath, and heartbeat."

"According to popular science, a human brain requires 20 watts of power to operate. Your brain generates enough electricity to power a light bulb."

"Your brain contains about 100 billion microscopic cells called neurons—so many it would take you over 3,000 years to count them all."

"Neurons send info to your brain at more than 150 miles (241 km) per hour."

"The structure of your brain changes every time you learn, as well as whenever you have a new thought or memory."

"It is well known that any exercise that makes your heart beat faster, like running or playing basketball, is great for your body and can even help improve your mood. But scientists have recently learned that for some time after you've exercised, your body produces a chemical that makes your brain more receptive to learning" (National Geographic, 2022)

"The historian of science may be tempted to exclaim that when paradigms change, the world itself changes with them."
Thomas Kuhn

Imagine a basketball, football, or soccer game to understand a paradigm better. The paradigm tells you there is a game, what type of game you are playing, the rules you must follow, and how to play it to win.

NEW PROGRAM CREATION - DELETE THE OLD PROGRAM

Reparadigming is changing to a new game, a new set of rules, a new way of playing the game, and a new program. And when the rules change, the whole game appears to be changing. Your world is transformed into the one you always wanted it to be.

Reparadigming means that the program installed in your brain written by people who loved you, your culture, environment, and genetic predisposition must be reprogrammed to fit the new you - the person you want to be and become. The new program will empower you to satisfy your needs, wants, and utmost desires.

If you are not getting what you want in life now, the program running you does not match the results you want. The old program must go. Reparadigming it's a must.

"Nothing is impossible to the mind. All its guidance and power are available to you. When you have fully realized THOUGHT CAUSES ALL, you will know there will never be any limits that you do not impose."
Uell Stanley Andersen

You are going to need to fix your old program or paradigm. Reparadigming means creating a new program, set of beliefs, rules, and regulations that will allow you to achieve the desired result. To do so, you must be aware enough to determine what programs are valid and valuable in your life and which must be thrown into the trashcan to be permanently deleted.

The only way to determine which ones must go and which should stay is by analyzing the results in different areas of your life. Remember that you are not run or controlled by one program; various programs control each area of our lives.

How many do we have? It's a great question to answer if anyone hasn't. We will not spend much time debating and philosophizing about the answer. Instead, we will mention but a few that the experts in the field of brain study, personal development, and success have determined to be the most important.

There are six main areas controlled by programs you still need to create. They are not listed in any order of importance. You can work on several simultaneously because, from personal experience, I can tell you that while all programs are independent, they run in harmony or work with one another as in a matrix or an orchestra. It's up to you to determine which one impacts your results the most and then start to create your program in that area of your life.

- Mind (mental)
- Body
- Family
- Society
- Finances
- Spirituality

Your task is to create a new program that will run on your internal computer or creative center and produce the desired results in each area of your life.

You can do this first by determining what you want. What do you really want? What is the result you truly and heartily desire? Yes, that's the new program's first and most important part. Remember that we are not asking you to think about how to do it or if you can get what you want. We certainly know that you can get anything you desire in this plane of existence since your creator equipped you with all the necessary tools to think, imagine, create, and achieve.

This is neither a discovery nor science fiction. It's as accurate as your first name and last name. The only thing limiting us from achieving greatness is the dreaded viruses of fear, unbelief, and lack of faith. These limitations are in the past, never to enter and contaminate our new programs.
Also, we will create an antivirus with the new program in case it is necessary to occasionally clean up and get rid of the bugs, just as any great programmer will do.

Creative Faith

"Thoughts become things. If you see it in your mind, you will hold it in your hand." Bob Proctor

They say that faith moves mountains. Is that possible, or is it just another story or telling from our parents, grandparents, and one of the many holy books? Let's dig deep into it and analyze and research the five-letter word that spring believes in, miracles, possibilities, myths, and realities. A term associated with spirituality, the unknown, the revered, a word or concept ignored and misunderstood by many.

The concept of faith is vital, essential, and has the utmost importance to dominate and master *The Art of Transfocreation*. This superpower is in you and is yours to manifest. Faith is not exclusive to religious beliefs, even though when most people listen to the word faith, their minds automatically think of God or religion. In that sense, faith is only one expression of faith; in a broader context, faith is the ability to imagine, visualize, and get whatever you desire.

The means and mechanisms of this are the secrets that will allow us to attain our heart desires. Of note, faith is the second most important, enticing, figurative, and powerful word after the most famous and significant one, which contains four letters: love.

> *"Now faith is the substance of things hoped for,*
> *the evidence of things not seen."* Hebrews 11:1(KJV)

In the book, *You Were Born Rich*, Bob Proctor –one of the best self-development teachers this world has ever seen - tells the story of Clarence Smithson and his concept of faith. Smithson has a unique quality, philosophy, and conviction regarding the idea he applies to his life. For him, faith is *"The ability to see the invisible and believe in the incredible, and that is what enables believers to receive what the masses think is impossible"* (Proctor, 2015).

This is a beautiful interpretation of faith. When I first heard this version of the word and analyzed it in detail, it had a profound impact and thus afforded a better understanding of its meaning.

Let's analyze the concept of faith from a scientific perspective and see how faith works practically. The mind is an infinite advanced center of creation and operations. Everything we see on the screen of our minds comes from our imagination. We can materialize or bring to reality any image on that screen.

In *The Power of the Subconscious Mind*, Dr. Joseph Murphy, Ph.D., D.D., asked what the master secret of all ages is. Is it the secret of atomic energy? Thermonuclear energy? The neutron bomb? Interplanetary travel?

Then he goes on to say. No, not any of these. Then what is this master secret? The answer is extraordinarily found in your subconscious mind, the last place where most people would seek it.

We have two minds: the conscious and the subconscious. When talking about faith, the operation mechanism is through our subconscious mind. When you think of something or a situation that you want, you can create and establish a firm belief or desire toward it. Imagine the intensity of the emotions you can generate that will transform into vibrations that, in terms, penetrate, transcend, fill, and activate the unlimited invisible powers that human senses cannot detect, but only by your higher faculties, i.e., the level of your consciousness and awareness (Murphy, 2020).

"Your subconscious mind will transmute into its physical equivalent
by the most direct and practical media available, any order given to it
in a state of BELIEF or FAITH that the order will be carried out."
(Hill, 2016).

The way the subconscious mind will transmit the message to be manifested is through vibrations. The type of vibration and its intensity will determine the result. One unique story of faith recorded in the Bible always amazes me. In Matthew 9:28-30, Jesus healed a blind man. What surprised me the most was what he told the blind man before performing the miracle.

And when He had come into the house, the blind men came to Him. And Jesus said to them, "Do you believe that I am able to do this?" They said to Him, "Yes, Lord." Then He touched their eyes, saying, "According to your faith, let it be to you." And their eyes were opened. And Jesus sternly warned them, saying, "See that no one knows it." Matthew 9: 28-30 (KJV)

This is a beautiful story and an example of how faith works. Everything we desire and believe in faith, we can achieve. Faith was the magic element used to heal the blind man. The belief that Jesus could heal him was how the miracle was made. *According to your faith, let it be to you!*

FAITH IS AN EMOTIONAL STATE

We know that our emotions and feelings control the level of vibrations. For example, say you just won ten million dollars off a lottery ticket that cost you one dollar, and you go home to tell your family. What do you think they perceive? Do you think they will notice something different in you before you tell them the news?

Yes, that is correct; they will perceive and notice something different in you by the positive vibrations you emanate. Even if your family were blind and could not see you enter the house, they would feel the difference created by your presence.

Our thoughts have energy, and we can increase their level with faith. Let's go back to the definition of Clarence Smithson on faith: *"The ability to see the invisible and believe in the incredible, and that is what enables believers to receive what the masses think is impossible"* (Proctor, 2015).

We can realize two things. First, we must be aware of our thoughts since our subconscious mind does not differentiate between negative and positive thoughts. When it comes to seeing the invisible, the invisible things we see or visualize must bring us good. It must be something that will spark our days and invoke happiness, joy, and satisfaction. For example, picture yourself fully healthy, traveling the world, or in your dream house or favorite car with your perfect companion. You are financially free, not having to worry about money ever again.

Believing in the incredible should be simple, even if you think it is not. Stop and consider how you would feel if you knew that you were created perfect and have all the tools needed to accomplish your wildest dreams.

Also, you know that everything is possible and can accomplish whatever you want. Would that certainty and assurance make you feel invincible, limitless, happy, and want to live at least two hundred years minimum to enjoy this wonderful world? I'm pretty sure that it would.

The impossible is possible for you NOW. Leave the incredible and incomprehensible to the unbelievers and doubters. Because you are reading this book, your awareness of infinite possibilities is growing, and a sense of invincibility fills your spirit. Remember that "it will be done to you according to your Faith"! It's just a matter of time before you materialize your goals using your faith.

YOU CAN CULTIVATE FAITH

Faith can be developed just like other faculty or ability. Do you believe it will be dark today after the sun sets and night comes? Your answer will be, "Yes, I have faith that night will come, and it will be dark.: Why is your belief that night will approach so strong? Maybe it is because you have experienced this event or because you understand the rules of nature regarding time: day and night.

We can conclude that faith is based on knowledge, understanding, and beliefs. Past events or history give us more confidence that the things we are hoping or waiting for will happen. Even if we don't understand the details of how the earth rotates on its axis, producing a specific position where the sun can reflect directly on it, and with that, the day will come. The science of this event guarantees that it will be done. Even a three-year-old can have faith and believe that he will go to sleep at night, and when he wakes up in the morning, it will no longer be dark.

In *Think and Grow Rich*, Napoleon Hills talks about developing faith. He states that faith is an emotional state that can develop and grow. This will not happen by causality or by itself; you must do it by using a principle. The best way to build faith is by using the same system used to materialize our desires into physical form, which is by autosuggestion.

Autosuggestion, also known as self-suggestion, is the repetition of affirmations so that the subconscious incorporates the affirmation thoughts into its framing of reality and protects this reality by actively working to achieve or maintain this end. By repeatedly suggesting to yourself that you have faith, you will develop it.

Predominant thoughts will always manifest in physical form. We become what we think about. The *law of attraction*, or *autosuggestion*, states that "like attracts like." That is nature's way of operating and why we must always remain confident and optimistic. When we have faith that we will get and accomplish our desires, we become unstoppable (Hill, 2016).

History is full of examples of people with great faith. Some of the most impressive historical heroes of faith are recorded in the Bible. Let us analyze some of them as phenomenal concepts of faith. This story can be found in Genesis chapters 12, 21, and 22.

Abraham is known as the father of faith. The biblical story tells that Abraham was 75 years old, and his wife Sarah was 65. Both were married but had no children when God first promised them they would conceive a child. Abraham will be called the father of many nations and Sarah, the mother of many nations.

Abraham was 100 years of age, and Sarah was 90 when she conceived Isaac, the child of the promise. Abraham was a wealthy and prosperous man. In those days, being childless was considered a curse or bad, especially for a male child who should continue the family legacy.

Now, this is where things get better. God told Abraham to sacrifice his son Isaac. Because Abraham's faith in God was so great, he offered his only son. Seconds before the sacrifice, God interceded and stopped Abraham from sacrificing his son. God provided a ram for the sacrifice.

"Now faith is the substance of things hopes for, the evidence of things not seen."
Hebrews 11:1 (KJV).

This sentence mesmerizes me every time I read it. Some of you might not believe or trust the Bible. (I see it as a library of many books written by credible authors who narrated the events of history to be proven by modern science.) Also, you might not believe in the existence of God as our creator. Do not worry since my intention is not to change your point of view and beliefs or bombard you with mine. I could not find a better source of proven knowledge to reference and rationalize the concept of faith.

Let's review the concept mentioned above of faith as a three-piece puzzle. Let's analyze each part independently to put it back together from the brighter light of understanding.

First piece: ***faith is the substance.*** What do you understand when you read, internalize, and analyze these four words? I understand that faith is equal to ***substance.***

But what is a substance? There are different definitions. The *Merriam-Webster* dictionary has different meanings: *essence: fundamental characteristic; physical material from which something is made, or which has discrete existence; an ultimate reality that underlies all outward manifestation and change.*

All definitions are acceptable, and you might choose one that resonates stronger in your heart. The one I find most appropriate that can be applied to the concept in the title of this book is *"the ultimate reality that underlies all outward manifestation and change."*

Wow, what a concept. Since faith is a substance, all things being equal, we can deduce that faith is the ultimate reality that underlies all outward manifestation and change. In simple words, faith or substance is a newly created reality that has the foundation of all outside visible expressed change. We can call it the process of materialization.

Continuing with the breakdown of faith, we move to the second piece of the puzzle: **of things hoped for**. I assume we don't need to get very technical or intellectual regarding the meaning of something you hope for. You can hope for many things: a world full of love, less pollution, better health, a happy family, lots of money, having your own business, finding your soul mate, a new career, a university degree, the house of your dreams, that new position in your current job, or just a great summer. In meek words, we hope for the things we desire or want to get and experience.

Now, let's break down the third piece of the concept of faith: **the evidence of things not seen.** I want to look closely into this third piece. What is the evidence? Let's go back to our dictionary reference: the words we know but sometimes like to verify that we know. Using the Merriam-Webster dictionary, we find the meaning of *evidence.*

Evidence*: an outward sign; something that furnished proof' one who bears witness; to be seen.*

In this third piece of the puzzle, we can understand that evidence is a sign or signal that shows or directs us to something. It is proof of the existence of something or serves as a witness to a specific event. Now that we have broken down the puzzle of faith into three pieces let's put it back together.

> *"Faith is the creation of a new reality that appears from-*
> *the idea of something you want and you are one-*
> *hundred percent certain you will receive."*
> Frank Ferguson

Now, have faith and start creating your new reality.

Jesus said to him, *"If you can believe, all things are possible to him who believes."* Mark 9:23 (KJV).

Your Superpower

As a kid, I'm pretty sure you fantasized about flying, fighting the bad guys, becoming invisible, saving people and animals, making a better world, saving the environment, or being indestructible. Have you ever thought of any superpower you would like to have if you were a superhero? I know I was, and it was fun. It still is…

Let me tell you something: You have superpowers already! When you finish this chapter, you will understand more about one. You will recognize this superpower and learn how to use it to achieve your goals and desires.

"Not every flying hero has a cape." Michael Jordan

The incredible thing about the power of *Transfocreation* is that everyone has it; although only a few people recognize it, only some know how to use it consciously. The superpower that transforms tangible and intangible things is a blessing given to us by our designer. To understand this power, let's review what makes this superpower possible.

UNIVERSAL LAWS

Our lives, the world, the solar system, and the universe are structured and organized. How the universe and our world function so perfectly are due to principles or laws that govern and control everything. God, our creator, works through these laws. Thus, these laws are immutable and never change.

Since the beginning, cultures such as the ancient African civilizations, old India, and the Greeks knew and understood these laws. They naturally used them by instinct in everything they did. These principles allowed them to develop incredible physical wonders and methods that are still admired today, such as the basis for construction, calculation, thinking, and healing.

The twelve laws are the Law of Divine Oneness, Law of Vibration, Law of Correspondence, Law of Attraction, Law of Inspired Action, Law of Perpetual Transmutation, Law of Cause and Effect, Law of Compensation, Law of Relativity, Law of Polarity, Law of Rhythm and Law of Gender.

If you learn, study, and understand these laws, you will find the solution to many of your questions regarding the situations you face on the way to achieving your ultimate life goals.

We will dive deep into one of these laws, the *Law of Polarity*. It contains a principle for discovering and developing one of your superpowers. "Everything is but one thing." The law expresses that all manifested things or situations have two sides, two aspects, two poles, and a pair of opposites—for example, hot-cold, hard-soft, love-hate, fear-courage, good-evil, night-day, poor-rich.

Not knowing it consciously, we talk about this law daily when we make the following statement: "There are two sides of the same coin, everything is and is not at the same time, and there are two sides of everything."

We can also understand this law when we look at the cardinal points. North is the opposite of south and east of west. There could not be a north without a south and no east without a west. Imagine traveling by plane and flying in a straight line, non-stop, in the direction of the east. At some point, you will end up in the west. Both east and west are on the same straight line; the only thing is that they are located in opposite directions.

Heat and cold are identical in nature, the difference a mere matter of degree. The thermometer shows many degrees of temperature, with the lowest point called cold, and the highest being hot. Light and darkness are poles of the same thing, with many degrees between them. Good and evil are not absolute; we call one end of the scale good and the other bad. Between the two sides of the good-bad scale are things "less bad" or "worse" than others, depending upon the position and direction you are looking at on the scale.

The same principle applies to the non-physical or mental aspect of things. "Love and hate" are generally regarded as feelings opposed to each other or entirely different. When using the Principle of Polarity, we find that there is no such thing as absolute love or hate. The two are merely expressions applied to opposites of the same emotion. What separates love from hate are the degrees of intensity.

If we have a love-hate scale represented by a line going from zero on the bottom and ten on the top, beginning at any point on the scale, we find "more love" or "less hate" as we ascend the scale, and "more hate" or "less love" as we descend. This is true no matter from what point, high or low, we may start.

By understanding this principle, we know that opposites can reconcile since their nature is the same. The universal reconciliation of opposites can be possible when we recognize and apply the Law of Polarity. At this point, you have a firm grip on the principle by which your superpower works, making it possible for you to *transfocreate* any situation, circumstance, or thing to your advantage to accomplish your goals and dreams.

Mastering this principle will allow you to manifest your superpower amazingly. Imagine if you could transform all the hate you have experienced to love by changing its polarity. How would your life be now?

Have you ever been afraid or experienced "fear" in your life? Perhaps it happened when making a decision that could transform your future and destiny. It could have been when giving a public speech or presentation, going for your dream job interview, or when the amount of money in your bank account was much lower than your monthly bills. This "fear" emotion you feel, or experience has its opposite: "courage."

YOU ARE COURAGEOUS!

Even if you don't think so, you are whom you are due to past experiences while living with or without fear. You are courageous. Yes, you are! You are a son or daughter of the omnipotent God! Awareness and using your superpower to transfocreate is the only thing stopping you from living a more prosperous life, where fear is just an illusion and courage characterizes you.

Suppose you can experience fear at a high level in a specific situation. In that case, you can also experience *courage* at a high level in that situation by making mental changes or a change of polarity. It means moving alongside the same scale from one side to the other or a change of degree.

You fully acknowledge this principle because of the mental pictures already in your brain with previews examples of love-hate, fear-courage, and good-bad. Know that each opposite is separated by degrees, and these degrees can be changed and manipulated by you.

Imagine driving late to work on a Monday morning in your brand-new Mercedes Benz GLE 350 Coupe Hybrid that you just got from the dealership the past Friday. You can still enjoy the new car smell and feel the perfect texture of your brown leather seats while listening to your favorite tune on the 900 watts 14-speaker Burmester sound system. Now, let's put your transfocreation superpower into practice by applying the Principle of Polarity.

All is going perfectly well, so you stop at an intersection at a red light. The light change to green, and you accelerate; just before leaving the interception, someone jumps a red light and hits the passenger side door.

You are not injured. Neither is the moron that caused the accident. But now you know that you will arrive late to work and have to manage all things related to car accidents.

You will have to wait for the police, deal with the insurance company, take the car to the dealership for repair, stay without your new vehicle for some time, and get a loaner while they fix yours. This entire scenario is processed in a blink of an eye, making you angry.

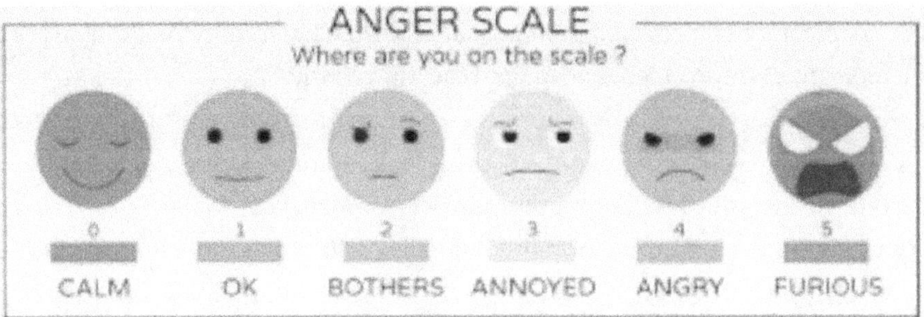

SUPERPOWER IN ACTION

In a situation like this, the usual or most common reaction will be anger and not its opposite, calm. Now is the time to use your superpower and *transfocreate* the situation.

As we know, angry-calm feelings are opposites of the same thing, on the same line or scale; they are separated by degrees. On a scale of 0 to 5, considering 0 to be very calm and 5 to be furious, where are you positioned in this situation? Let's say you are in 4, which means you are considerably angry.

We will now break the situation into pieces by analyzing all things involved. First, you are not hurt, and that is a blessing. Your car is a secure, solid, and well-manufactured vehicle - the best on the market with safety features like the Mercedes-Benz PRE-SAFE® system that automatically activates if an accident is about to happen. This safety feature takes preventative measures to ensure you and your passengers are safe. You were brilliant by choosing to own a protective safe with four wheels (German-made).

The car's features are fascinating factors. You were going to be late anyway, and anyone can have a car accident in the scope of life. Your boss will not fire you because of it; instead, he and your colleagues will be more empathetic and cover your responsibilities.

SELF-DEFENSE MECHANISM

Remember that you were going to arrive late. To be angry, your body must become tense, your muscles activated, and your blood must flow faster than usual due to the acceleration of your heartbeat. This body reaction is the perfect defense mechanism that could save your life; for example, take a scenario where a bear chases you.
All physical information provided is beneficial. If we had been conscious and aware of it at the moment of the accident, we might react differently.

But you were not the one who caused the accident. Your driver's license, traffic tickets, and car insurance will not be compromised. Also, your insurance will assist with transporting your car to the repair shop. They will provide a loaner when your brand-new vehicle is being repaired.

Say the person who caused the accident was a very prominent business owner of an enterprise with which your company does business. He was on his way to the airport. He was late and stressed about missing his flight to Japan for a crucial business meeting.

Your body and mind are yours; they should serve you, not the other way around. Many reactions to situations are automatic; they happen without our command. We can learn to control ourselves and not react with our primitive brain (survival instincts), which protects us from an imminent threat or life-and death-situation. We should therefore respond and refrain from reacting.

When our higher mind triggers a response, it is more probable that there will be a positive and more convenient outcome. Past experiences are stored in our brains in the form of programs that usually influence our reactions. These programs are formed and installed in our subconscious with or without authorization and awareness.

When an event triggers a specific feeling, these programs are deployed into action in a split second, sometimes causing more harm than good. In the case of the car accident, the program made the driver react with "Level 4 Anger,"- referring to the anger scale.

Because you understand the Law of Polarity and know that anger and calm are on the same line, we need to move the scale from anger to calm to control the intensity between anger and calmness.

How you do this might be your initial reaction to my statement.

There are many techniques you can use. To mention a few, take a deep abdominal breath through your nose and exhale through your mouth several times, count from ten to one while deeply breading, think and focus on a possible positive outcome from the accident, visualize yourself calm and relax, drop your shoulders to relax your body, and repeat a mantra a song or poem that mentally calms you down.

We can mention many other techniques to relax and change from anger to calmness, but the idea is for you to try these or other methods and define the best. With constant practice and repetition, you will master one or several, and with that, you can change the degrees between the opposites of any emotion, situation, mental state, or feeling.

This was just a quick and simple example of how applying simple techniques could change the perspective and outcome of difficult situations.

By being aware of the Law of Polarity and how opposites are the same when we look at them on a scale, we can now have a different approach to dealing with challenging scenarios that life brings us. Your superpower to influence, manipulate, and change outcomes are now in your hands to be used in your quest for a better and happier life.

After you applied the relaxing technique mentioned above, you were able to calm down and move the anger scale from angry to ok (4 to 1); with that, the traffic accident became more manageable, your stress levels decreased, and you were able to think clearly.

NEW REALITY

In a short time, what could be an outburst of toxic substances released by stress hormones, a product of our fight or flight mechanism, could be stopped and controlled. With this, minimizing adverse effects to our health also prevents triggering our animal's aggressive instinct that could put us in a legal situation if we decide to follow this animal instinct and escalate our anger until we physically engage in aggression and end up sued or in jail.

After we could relax and decrease the anger scale from 4 to 1, we could engage in a civilized way and have a conversation with the driver that created the accident. He apologized and explained what made the situation. He was going late to the airport and was stressed that he would miss the flight for his business trip to Japan.

After a short conversation and exchange of contact information, you realize that the offender is one of your biggest clients, and you gain his confidence and trust due to how you manage the incident. After a couple of weeks, your company was able to close a big deal with the offender and his company because you built a more personal relationship after the car accident. With that, you gain a bonus.

Wow, what a way to *transfocreate* a problematic situation into a great and juicy bonus!

Now, go and use your superpower and become a superhero for yourself and others.

"Never say never because limits, like fears, are often just an illusion."
Michael Jordan

CHAPTER 6

Self-image

Experts argue that self-image is the critical factor in the results produced by a person during his lifetime. Self-image is also one of the most important discoveries in the field of psychology. Many schools of thought have different meanings and definitions of what it is. It's not hard to comprehend that the word itself gives us a good hint as to its essence: the image you have of yourself or how you see yourself. I'm confident that you have your understanding.

We all have a mental picture of how we see ourselves, and it does not matter if you are aware of it. In other words, you have an image of whom you think you are. This image is what we use to build our personality, character, and belief system.

Past and present experiences and interactions with your inner and outer world create your beliefs. Each feeling of success, disappointment, satisfaction, embarrassment, or ridicule, beginning from childhood, and how people respond to you creates this mental image. It then becomes something genuine to you; it does not matter if it's a positive or negative image. Once constructed, it will run automatically as part of who you are.

As you mature during your lifetime, this image is consolidated and framed automatically in your subconscious in an effortless and non-conscious way for most people. This process has a few exceptions, but it's the norm in most cases.

A young child who is well nurtured, loved, and appreciated by his family, who always receives complements for his great physical looks, good behavior, and intelligence, will see himself as a beautiful, intelligent, and loving child every time he looks at the mirror - also his inner mental mirror.

On the other side, if a child is raised in an environment that is not supportive, he is constantly yelled at, never receives a good complement, and is continuously mocked due to his appearance, this child will start viewing himself as something ugly, not worthy, unwanted and with no value when he looks in a mirror and, of course, his inner mental mirror.

"We become what we think about." Earl Nightingale

Why is a book that talks about the concept of *transfocreation* have an entire chapter dedicated to self-image? It might suggest to the reader that there is a correlation between one's self-image, how you view the world, how the world looks at you, and the process of transfocreation. Indeed, you are correct; there is a considerable correlation between self-image and the concept of *transfocreation.*

In 1960, Dr. Maxwell Maltz wrote a book entitled, *Psych-Cybernetics.* Maltz was a plastic surgeon who discovered that many of his patients, after receiving a new look following plastic surgery - either to correct an imperfection or fix something due to a trauma or accident – saw their personalities and behavior change mainly in a very peculiar and expected way. In other cases, even when he performed his best surgery and the patient was transformed to become almost perfect, this patient did not experience any change in behavior, self-esteem, and personality (Maltz, 1989).

Those peculiar cases led this plastic surgeon to study and development of a new way of performing surgeries without a scalpel or a surgical knife. He realized that even though he could modify the patient's external image if the patient could not change their inner image, the surgery would not attain its intended purpose. In most cases, it uplifts the patient's confidence, self-esteem, performance, and ability to cope with day-to-day life.

According to Dr. Maltz, self-image is vital to achieving a fulfilling and successful life. There are two main factors to be considered. First, everything you do, how you feel, and how you behave cohere with your self-image. Second, self-image can be modified or changed; you can transform your life into a new and better one (Maltz, 1989).

FAILURE TO CHANGE

Most of us have tried to change our habits, behaviors, and personality traits with little to no success. How often do you or people you know set a goal to get in top shape when the new year starts? They enroll in a fitness center to find that they succumb to frustration in less than a month or two with no tangible results. Then they just quit, thinking negative things about their body and their ability to be disciplined enough to get in shape.

Or you may know someone who has been trying to learn a second language for years. They enrolled in all types of courses that promised the perfect and most innovative formula to learn a new language, to feel frustrated because it did not work. They spent their money, time, and effort with slight improvement. What is the main reason for these behavioral patterns?

There are many factors behind why these patterns are so common. It is interesting to see how motivational techniques, inspirational talks, self-talk, and positive thinking can do the trick for a short period. Yet eventually, the person crawls back into their previous habitual, unfulfilled self.

You should feel very fortunate and happy today because you will no longer be one of these people. It's a new dawn for you, a time to transfocreate, change, and achieve. There is an explanation and solution for this. Let's start with the reasoning.

THE INTERNAL MIRROR EFFECT

Most people try to change their external aspect, not the core or main one. For example, a person trying to learn a new language tells himself, "This time, I will not quit; I will do well, I will be very discipline, and I will learn a second language." Notice that the focus is on external circumstances and the perimeter of the self, not on the center or central aspect.

When learning a new language, the center or central aspect this person should consider is their image of themselves. Does the person usually tell himself, "I'm not good at languages? I don't have the facility or skill to learn a new language easily. My friends took the same courses, and now they are proficient, but I'm not." How do they express themself about language learning when talking to a friend or their new language instructor?

If you listen to what the person thinks of his "self-image" when learning a new language, you will see that the problem has to do with self-image; it is not a learning problem. If he changes his image to one more in tune with language learning, his learning problems will dissipate, and he will learn the new language quickly and easily.

Let's say the person decided to change his old image and paint a new one: "I love to learn new languages, and they come easy. Every day, I learn more and more. I'm becoming very good at learning this new language".

If they can view themselves as a good language learner, a great student, and someone who learns fast, their ability to learn a new language will surely improve since they have replaced the old image with a new one.

You can't think positively about a situation if you think negatively of yourself in a specific case. When you change how you see yourself in a particular scenario, you will quickly change anything related to that scenario.

Prescott Lecky, one of the pioneers of self-image psychology, had a theory. He stated that if a student has difficulties learning a specific subject, it could be due to the student's point of view. Lecky thought that if he could change the student's self-concept and make him believe that learning a subject is not inconsistent with his image, his attitude could also change. If the student could be induced to change his self-definition, his learning ability should also change (Prescott, 1945).

Lecky tested his theory with a student who misspelled 55 words out of 100. Thus, he failed his class that school year. But the following year, he had an average of 91 and became one of the best spellers in the school. Another student dropped out due to bad grades, entered a new university, and became a straight "A" student.

After three talks with the school counselor, a girl who had flunked Latin four times finished with a grade of 84, a boy whom a testing bureau told that he had no aptitude for English won an honorable mention the next year and was granted a literary prize (Prescott, 1945).

The trouble with these students was not that they were dumb or lacking in fundamental aptitudes. The problem was an inadequate self-image ("I don't have a mathematical mind"; "I'm just naturally a poor speller"). They "identified" with their mistakes and failures. Instead of saying, "I failed that test" (factual and descriptive), they concluded, "I am a failure." Instead of saying, "I flunked that subject," they said, "I am a flunk-out."

These few real-life recorded scientific studies shed much light on the validity and importance of having an acceptable, realistic, and positive self-image. In all the histories of people who failed or succeeded, their self-image was the common factor that made or broke them. You can learn a great lesson from this on your way to transfocreating your new life. How you see "you" will determine the type of life and degree of happiness you will experience.

Putting this theory into practical use, we can now understand that whatever you want to create, change, or achieve in life starts with the image you have made and applied to what you want to become. A person can have multiple images for corresponding areas of his life.

For example, you can have a self-image of a daughter, a mother, an athlete, a student, a professional, a cook, a dancer, or a lover. It does not matter what you are into or do; there is always an image of how you see yourself in every situation.

A professional tennis player must see herself as one of the best in the world before she can be considered to play in a Wimbledon tournament. The image of someone who wants to become a bestselling author must have a self-image of a great writer, someone with the knack to formulate sentences and expressions and transmit ideas.

One who can transport people to mental and physical places, who can create mental images with words and achieve a defined purpose. The trick is to be aware of this fact to become the best version of yourself that you can be.

"Having seen the end, you have willed the means for the realization of the end."
Thomas Troward

SELF-IMAGE CREATION

Your imagination creates your self-image. You have to first think of the specific attributes of the image that will assist you in attaining a particular purpose or goal you have in mind. Then you must create the image based on the qualities required to achieve your goal. After you have completed the picture, it is essential that you internalize it, own it, and feel it as part of you. It would be best if you believed that you are this new self-image. Soon enough, you will start behaving, acting, and making decisions based on the new self-image that is controlling your life subconsciously and automatically.

This process is similar to a system or practice used in the mechanical, computer, design, electronic, and software industries known as "Reverse Engineering." It's a method in which one attempts to understand through deductive reasoning how a previously made device, process, system, or piece of software accomplishes a task with little (if any) insight into exactly how it does so. We will explore this technique and its application in another chapter.

"One of the greatest weaknesses a person can have is a lack of self-confidence. When we have faith that we absolutely can and will attain what we most desire, we are unstoppable".
Napoleon Hill

Personal Healing Powers

You are powerful beyond imagination, and that power is abundantly infinite. Your body is a unique self-healing mechanism. This mechanism is a superpower in itself. Knowing how it works and being able to control it is one of the most important things to learn. In this chapter, we will begin understanding the command center that regulates our healing, not only the recovery of our bodies but how to use this power to heal others even if they are 10,000 kilometers away.

"The good news is that the moment you decide that what you know is more important than what you have been taught to believe, you will have shifted gears in your quest for abundance. Success comes from within, not from without." Ralph Waldo Emerson

The traditional education system was created to develop practical professionals in different fields for society to produce, grow, and sustain itself. I see nothing wrong with that, but it's vital that you dedicate your time and resources to understanding, comprehension, and development of yourself. It's crucial to have an open mind regarding our bodies and mind.

This should be done via theoretical and, most importantly, practical knowledge. Apply and experience everything you learn to be convinced that you are on the correct path of personal development and becoming enlightened.

SELF-HEALING

From ancient times, humanity was firmly convinced that a power deep inside us could heal our bodies and minds. This power could be called upon to lessen suffering and create a better world. History proves that this power exists and has dramatically improved people's lives. This self-healing power works if you are aware of it and also if you are not.

Since the beginning of times, healers performed most healings; they possessed the ability to cure different diseases and problems. With time, healers have had remarkable results all around the world, even where medicine or doctors are not able to perform. Sometimes, we see magical cures and ask ourselves how this could be possible.

The answer is due to the blind belief and faith that patients have in the healer. They trust, respect, and believe that the healer will help the sick person release the healing powers residing in their subconscious mind, the one that cures them and creates the miracle.

We can trace this healing concept to the bible.

"Therefore, I tell you, whatever you ask for in prayer, believe that you have received it, and it will be yours." Mark 11:24

Let's analyze the concept of prayer. What is prayer? In the Oxford Dictionary, prayer is "a solemn request for help or expression of thanks addressed to God or an object of worship." The Bible tells us to ask in prayer and believe that we have already received it; then, it will manifest to you or in you.

Interesting indeed! When we pray, we connect to the frequency of our creator; by doing so, we can achieve anything we can ask for. Prayer, in other words, is a form of communication with our creator, God, or what we believe to be the source of creation. But how does this communication happen? It is not physical communication; instead, it's a mental or spiritual connection. We must understand that everything is energy, and God is energy.

Our faith bonds this process of receiving what we ask for in prayer. We must be sure that we will get what we ask for. Just as the previews verse of Mark 11:24 says, *"Believe that you have already received it, then it will manifest to you or in you."* It could not be crystal clear.

Now we must understand the process of praying. Do you think God will descend from the heavens and fulfill our requests when we pray and believe? Maybe not, for sure not. God doesn't need to fall from the sky since he is God. One of God's qualities is his omnipresence. That means He is already everywhere; He is in us, and we share his spiritual makeup.

This book is not intended to get into religious beliefs or theology. The concept of God was not very clear to me for a long time. I'm sure it's still an abstract thought for many people, not easy to understand. Still, at the same time, personal healing powers are linked to our higher nature (spirit) created by God, or as some people and the scientific community call it, energy.

Since God is in all and all is in God, we can connect to our inner selves when we pray. God built this self in a certain way to enjoy powerful means by which healing, miracles, and amazing things are done.

We already have the capability of healing others and ourselves; it is not something we acquire but something we learn to use. All of us have superpowers ready to be manifested in our subconscious minds. Yes, our subconscious minds are the link to the supernatural forces of the universe, which are, in turn, connected directly to God. By using the power of our subconscious minds and by suggestion, we can alter and manipulate all our bodies' cells; that ability can go beyond the physical self.

We can alter or stimulate objects and other people even if they are 10,000 km away. The distance will not matter because when we learn how to use this power, we connect to the infinite channel of energy that permeates and penetrates all the interspaces of the universe.

"Every thought-seed sown or allowed to fall into the mind, and to take root there, produces its own, blossoming sooner or later into the act, and bearing its own fruitage of opportunity and circumstance. Good thoughts bear good fruit, bad thoughts bad fruit."
James Allen

SUBCONSCIOUS MIND POWERS

From ancient times before science was conceived and what we understand now as modern medicine was created, healers knew how to tap into their inner powers. The power of suggestion was very effective, primarily if the healer was held in high regard and respected by the ill person. The same thing happens now with doctors and patients. Doctors tap into their self-healing powers, consciously or unconsciously.

This concept is not a new one. From 1910 to 1919, Dr. Hippolyte Bernheim, professor of medicine at Nancy, France, presented the fact that the "suggestion" of the physician to the patient was transferred through the subconscious mind. Bernheim showed that the power of faith and expectancy on the part of the patient acts as a powerful subconscious tool of suggestion. (Bernheim, 1919).

If more doctors understood this concept, they would see a higher patient recovery rate while avoiding dangerous surgeries or procedures that may not benefit their patients. When it comes to medications, it is better not even to talk about them. But I can assure you, using scientific proof, that most people are taking many drugs they shouldn't.
Recent scientific discoveries are just catching up with this reality. They are starting to understand the human brain and its mental self-healing powers. Various laboratory experiments have been conducted to test self-healing using a control group.

A control group refers to participants who do not receive the drug or treatment but receive a different standard of care or a placebo. Note that the control and actual group don't know who receives what. Sometimes, these experiments are so well done that not even the person administering the drug or placebo knows who is receiving which one. This method is called double blinding.

Many of these experiments conclude that patients receiving the actual drug and those receiving the placebo have the same effects. How can this be possible? Scientists can only account for the role of suggestion or the patient's thinking, called autosuggestion.

A mind is a potent tool and internal physician. Our subconscious mind can work miracles both inside and outside our bodies. It would be best if you remembered that you are always powerful. Also, that healing power is inside of you - in your subconscious mind. Healing and faith go hand in hand; if you plant a seed or idea in your mind of a result you wish to achieve, all you need to do is water and nourish it with expectancy, and you will get the intended result. This is a law, and we accept that laws rule our universe.

All diseases begin in the mind, they say. Nothing develops in the body unless there is a corresponding mental formation. There is only one process of healing, and that is faith. There is only one healing power through which miracles and healing happen, namely, the subconscious mind. It's how God connects to our spiritual selves and does His work in and from us.

"The body is the servant of the mind. It obeys the operations of the mind, whether they be deliberately chosen or automatically expressed. At the bidding of unlawful thoughts, the body sinks rapidly into disease and decay; at the command of glad and beautiful thoughts, it becomes clothed with youthfulness and beauty.
James Allen

Forgiveness (Clear and Restart)

Forgiveness is like being full of sweat after a cross-country race and then enjoying a warm shower. You feel new after the miraculous effect of the water, plus what soap and a sponge can do for your body. You become different; you feel free, clean, and relaxed. You are ready to restart your current activities with renewed energy and poise.

Have you been forgiven for a debt, wrongdoing, mistake, or sin? How did it make you feel? We all have been forgiven at one point along life's journey. Being forgiven is excellent, like getting a gorilla off your shoulders. Without that heavy weight, you can resume your journey and breathe again. You feel alive with restored energy to move on toward your destiny.

There are significant connotations regarding forgiveness. A simple look into forgiveness might show that it's something insignificant, but this subject goes way beyond forgiving others and ourselves.

There are long-lasting effects or repercussions from ignoring the severity and magnitude of the concept. A lack of forgiveness has been responsible for the great ruin of people, families, businesses, and society. Every aspect of our social structure is affected by forgiveness, and this happens with or without our knowledge.

Do not underestimate the role forgiveness has in the human playground of this world. The fact that you are thinking and remembering both your past and present experiences of forgiveness is a testament to your awakening, hopefully leading to a better, richer, and more fulfilled life. It should improve your circle of influence for generations to come.

Philosophy, science, theology, and history have analyzed, recorded, and provided vast information on forgiveness. We will endeavor to understand the best methods to apply forgiveness to ourselves and others.

BIBLE TEACHINGS ON FORGIVENESS

One of the most known biblical teachings on forgiveness is the Lord's Prayer. In Matthew chapter six, the disciples are amazed and surprised that Jesus is always praying to God, and they ask him to teach them how to pray. Jesus then proceeds to provide them with what is known today as the Lord's Prayer:

"This, then, is how you should pray: Our Father in heaven, hallowed be your name, your kingdom come, your will be done, on earth as it is in heaven. Give us today our daily bread. **And forgive us our debts as we forgive our debtors.** *And lead us not into temptation, but deliver us from the evil one. For thine is the kingdom, and the power and the glory, forever. Amen".*   Matthew 6: 9-13 (KJV)

If we analyze this prayer in more detail, we find that the first thing Jesus recognizes and acknowledges is his *"Father in heavens"* – God, the supreme creator of everything with no beginning or end. Then he provided the scope of God's omnipotence and omnipresence in the entire universe. *"Your will be done, on earth as it is in heavens."* He follows by telling us who provides everything we need as humans. *"Give us today our daily bread."* Then Jesus expresses the need for forgiveness, not only the one we need, but the forgiveness we must provide to others. *"And forgive us our debts, as we also have forgiven our debtors."*

Why did Jesus touch the subject of forgiveness in the first ever-recorded teaching on how to pray? Is forgiveness so crucial that Jesus reminded us to incorporate it into our daily prayers? I say, yes, this is true emphatically. But why? I guess it will remain a mystery, but as we use our imagination, we could agree that even if we don't have an answer to the "why," we can concur on the "for what."

When someone forgives us, we feel good; we feel free. Imagine losing your job a couple of months ago due to an unexpected disease, and you owe your bank $500,000. The loan was due two months ago, but you could not come up with at least the minimum to keep the bank happy. If you can't repay this loan in a few days, the bank will take your house and car. What will follow would be an unhappy wife and kids, dissatisfaction, culpability, and more stress, leading to health deterioration and, finally, a broken family.

No one would like to be in or even dream about such a situation. The time has come, and the bank is ready to take over your house and car. They will remove you from your home in 24 hours. When you think all is lost, you receive a call from the bank manager with news that your debt was paid in full and you will not have to move out of your house and give back your car.

How would you feel? I'm sure you will ask the bank how this turn of events was possible. I would. The bank manager tells you that someone stepped into the bank and decided to cancel your debt in full. The person chose to remain anonymous. You will not have to pay it back or worry about it anymore. In short, you are free.

This example is an excellent instance of the feeling we might experience if our financial debts were forgiven. Knowing that you could lose your material possessions and your family in the process was no doubt terrifying. I'm pretty sure that after the debt payment, your health made a quantum leap improvement overnight. Your wife became the loving and caring person you fell in love with, and your sweet kids are smiling again while playing in the backyard.

We could use many other scenarios of forgiveness, such as a jail sentence, wrongdoing made to your best friend, a traffic ticket, or infidelity in a relationship. The feeling of freedom, a new beginning, being able to sleep at night, and releasing a heavy burden off your shoulders is tremendous.

FORGIVING OURSELVES

After you knew and acknowledged that you did something wrong, a time when you messed up, did you experience an internal war in your mind? You were aware of all the pain you had created - how you let others and yourself down. That feeling is terrible, but I'm sure we all have experienced this feeling of guilt and the loss of our will to go on.

When we are in these situations, the world loses its color and looks cloudy and gray. You feel shame, have a heavy heart, lose your appetite, and have low energy; things are just not the same. You feel motionless as a body with no soul. All these emotions and feelings are well deserved, one would think. "Now is my time to pay, and all these feelings, restless nights, depression, or even self-inflicted punishment are the price to pay."

We could even feel so deserving of the consequences of our wrong actions that we become our punishers. We are the accused and the avenger at the same time.

STOP; you must stop thinking this way. Remember that we can be our worse critics and punishers. That wrong mental approach turns into self-pity and self-scouring. Not only do we punish our current mistakes, but we can punish our entire lives. How is this possible? Let's analyze it from a psychological and scientific perspective.

Dr. Joseph Murphy, in "The power of the subconscious mind," talks about how life always forgives. If you consume contaminated food, life forgives you and causes you to vomit to preserve you. If you cut your finger, your subconscious intelligence begins to repair it by building new cell bridges over the cut.

If you burn your hand, the "Life Principle" reduces the edema and congestion and generates new skin cells. In general, life holds no resentment against you, and it is always forgiving you.

Life brings you back to health, vitality, harmony, and peace if you cooperate with nature. Negative, hurtful memories, bitterness, and ill will impede the free flow of the Life Principle in you.

You were created with a marvelous self-repair mechanism. Part of this mechanism functions automatically, flowing from your subconscious mind. By contrast, your conscious mind thinks about curing your body by learning and practicing self-forgiveness (Murphy, 2020).

Forgiving ourselves has the most significant impact on the way we feel and our actions and results in life. We don't have control over other people's forgiveness, but we do have control over us forgiving others and incredibly forgiving ourselves. This chapter analyzes three kinds of forgiveness: forgiving others, forgiving ourselves, and accepting others forgiving you.

Others can forgive us for our past mistakes, but if we don't assume control of our minds and do the necessary work on ourselves, we will live our lives with resentment, low self-esteem, and a negative self-image. This can lead to the erroneous programming of our subconscious mind, resulting in continual self-sabotage that leads to an unhappy and unfulfilled life for you and your loved ones.

Remember that awareness is vital to self-development. The primary purpose of this book is to spark awareness and consciousness. After that spark is on, you will begin a new journey by putting thought into actions that will lead to a pleasant, prosperous, and happy life.

FORGIVING OTHERS

As crucial as it is to forgive ourselves for acquiring the image of the person we are meant to become, forgiving others is critical to unleashing universal blessings.

It is in our complete control to forgive others for the wrongs they have done to us. It is simple: *"Do to others as you would like others to do to you."* Why should someone else forgive you if you are unwilling to forgive others?

There is an exciting story in the bible in Matthew 18: 23-35 of a man who was the servant of a king. This man owed the king ten thousand gold coins. Since he could not pay, he was ordered to sell all he had, including his wife and kids, to repay his debt. When the servant heard this, he fell on his knees before the king. "Be patient with me," he begged, "and I will pay back everything." The king took pity on the servant, canceled his debt, and freed him.

When the servant went home, he found that one of his servants owed him one hundred silver coins. He grabbed him by the neck and began to choke him, demanding, "Pay back what you owe me!" His servant fell on his knees and begged, "Be patient with me, and I will pay it back." This man refused to forgive his servant and then had the servant thrown in prison until he could pay him back.

When other servants saw what had happened, they became angry and went to the king and told him the news. The king became very angry with the servant and called him. When he came, the king said the servant. "You wicked servant. I canceled all your debt because you begged me to. Shouldn't you have mercy on your fellow servant just as I had on you? In anger, the king sent him to prison to be tortured until he could pay back all he owed.

The lesson is straightforward: in life, there are times when we will be in the position of the king who forgave his servant, while at other times, we will be in the role of the servant who could have forgiven his servant but decided not to. Where do you fit in this story? Are you the servant who was forgiven but could not forgive? Decide today who you will be.

Forgiving others is a matter of helping others so that someone will help you in the future, one might think. That is dandy and good, but take advantage of the bigger picture here. Forgiving others is fundamental for mental and physical health. It would be best to forgive others for living a healthy and happy life.

> *"To forgive is to give something for. Give love, peace, joy, wisdom, and all the blessings of life to the other, until there is no sting left in your mind. This is really the acid test of forgiveness."* Joseph Murphy

ADVERSE EFFECTS OF NOT FORGIVING

In different fields of medicine, such as psychology, psychiatry, and psychosomatic, it has been demonstrated that forgiveness is rooted in resentment, blame, guilt, anger, and other negative emotions. These feelings cause many diseases, from arthritis to cardiac conditions. We could write a book about the effects in the ledger of mental disorders.

Not forgiving others affects your present health, of course. It's time to do some self-analysis or soul-searching and begin to transfocreate your minds and bodies with the power of forgiveness. All you need to do is be willing - decide and then do it. If you desire to forgive, you have already won the battle. The rest is just execution.

One critical point about forgiving is that you don't need to become best friends or socialize when you forgive someone for whatever reason. Just root it out of your heart and mind; in other words, try to forget.

People probably say, "I forgive, but don't forget." That type of forgiveness is hypocritical and not sincere. The positive health effects attained from this type of forgiveness are then minimal.

"Try to forget" is the key phrase. It might seem impossible to forget, but that should be the goal. Suppose we keep a fresh memory of all the lousy someone has done to us, constantly talk about it to others, or replay the images in our brain theater. In that case, we are poisoning ourselves with negative emotional vibrations. You are tuning into a dark and lousy frequency that will only affect you negatively. It's like preparing a poison to kill someone but drinking it yourself.

I will share a very easy, effective, and simple method described by Dr. Joseph Murphy in one of his best-selling books, "The Power of your Subconscious Mind."

Sit or get in a comfortable position in a quiet place, then relax by taking five deep breaths. Affirm the following statement, "I completely and freely forgive (mention the name of the person, institution, or situation you will forgive). I release them mentally and spiritually. I completely forgive everything connected with the matter. I am free, and they are free. It's a wonderful feeling. It's my day of amnesty. I release anyone and everyone who has ever hurt me, and I wish everyone health, happiness, peace, and all the blessings of life. I do this freely, joyously, and lovingly, and whenever I think of the person or people who hurt me, I say, "I have released you, and all the blessings of life are yours" I am free, and you are free. It's wonderful."

God never punishes. The man punishes himself with his false concept of God, life, and the universe. His thoughts are creative, and he creates his misery. To understand all is to forgive all.

"When a man understands the creative law of his own mind, he ceases to blame other people and conditions for making or marring his life. He knows that his own thoughts and feelings create his destiny. Furthermore, he knows that externals are not the causes and conditioners of his life and experiences. To think that others can mar your happiness, that you are the football of a cruel fate that you must oppose and fight others for a living— all these and others like them are untenable when you understand that thoughts are things. The Bible says the same thing.

"For as a man thinketh in his heart, so is he." Proverbs 23:7" (Murphy, 2020)

CHAPTER 9

Success Feeling

The feeling of success and accomplishment is a beautiful feeling to have. When you succeed at something, you feel strong and full of courage, and your confidence increases. We live in a goal-driven society that can and will differentiate a winner from a loser. Because of this, most people are working hard to achieve their dreams and become successful.

Nobody wants to be a loser, but not everyone can be successful according to traditional thinking. You are not part of the common masses that sets limits on their unlimited potential and creativity by thinking inside the box.

Because of this, we begin with the premise and conviction that you and everyone in this world have the potential to be successful at something. But that's the way you *think* now. Your new reality is to think outside the box and generate a quantum leap beyond your wildest dreams of success and achievement.

What type of experiences, lessons, habits, disciplines, and mental conditions would you like to model - your life or sports career? The answer is straightforward: to "the best." Life and sports have parallels; we can transfer experiences, lessons, habits, disciplines, and mental states from sports to our daily lives and vice versa.

High-performance people or high-performance athletes have specific qualities that differentiate them from the average person. What sets them apart is the physical superiority or IQ you think they might possess - which is not always true. What sets them apart is their mental attitude. They are just wired differently. Super success in life and sports is available to anyone willing to put in the time and effort, i.e., the person willing to pay the price in advance.

We possess such an incredible system, commonly known as the duality of the mind and the body, that, in tandem, will help us become super successful. This is the intention behind writing this book, and it should be your belief that once you have finished reading, studying, and applying the concepts, that will *transfocreate* a new and better you. You will become a high-performance and super-successful person if that's what you want, or you can improve in a specific area. The person you want to become is there but maybe dormant. Just wake them up, release, liberate, and unleash them into the physical world. Yes, you can, and you will.

WHAT IS SUCCESS FEELING?

Human beings are emotional. You and everyone you have encountered and will ever encounter - no matter their race, social status, creed, IQ level, or gender - are ruled by feelings and emotions. Love, compassion, fear, gratitude, faith, failure, invincibility, hope, and many other human attributes are manifested through feelings. We live in an internal sea of emotions and an external ocean of emotions called society.

How we think generates feelings; those feelings then make us act a certain way. In turn, those actions produce results, good or bad.

Knowing this fact, now we should ask ourselves, who controls our thoughts, emotions, and feelings? Are we programmed to be controlled by people, situations, and circumstances, or are we the masters of our destinies, controlling our thoughts, feelings, emotions, actions, and results? I'm pretty sure you know the answer.

Success feeling is nothing other than the satisfaction you get when you achieve, accomplish, or win something. For example: when your favorite sports team wins a championship; when you get a good grade in school; when you get the "*Yes, I will*" from your significant other after you propose; when you get that dream job or promotion you worked so hard for; when you buy your first house; when you get the car you desired; or when you lose weight and get that healthy, strong, and gorgeous body you always want. In general, it is when you achieve a goal.

SUCCESS MECHANISM

Thinking and imagining our goals' outcomes and feeling as a positive and present possibility is essential. You and everyone else possess an internal success mechanism that will accomplish goals and subsequently generate the feeling of success. To experience this feeling, it is essential first to define the objective and the result you expect. Once you do this, your success mechanism will automatically provide how to accomplish that goal.

"Imagination is more important than knowledge." Albert Einstein

Your mind's automatic success mechanism cannot differentiate between real and imagined success; the same goes for real and imagined failure. It would be best if you imagined yourself always attaining a positive outcome no matter your current life circumstances. Many super-successful people talk about the winning or success feeling they experience before closing a big deal or winning a significant game. That attitude is what separates winners from losers.

NERVOUS SYSTEM

Success does not happen by chance since we must program our minds for success. When our minds are prepared for success, we usually succeed at something. We do this by experiencing the feeling of success before it happens. A simple trick can lead us to victory.

When you feel confident and optimistic, it's more likely that you will act in a way conducive to success. Feeling successful and confident alone will not guarantee success, but it's a sign that something good is in the making. It's like when the sky turns gray, clouds start to appear, and rain follows. The sky turning grey and clouds appearing do not guarantee rain, but we all know there is a good chance.

You might be thinking, what happens if I am never successful and never have the winning feeling for something specific? How can I be confident? The answer is above your shoulders in your cerebral cortex.

Since humans are unique, our brains and minds are developed in a way that rivals any supercomputer or AI (artificial intelligence) technology. Using our higher faculties – imagination and visualization - we can produce an image or mini video of us succeeding at our intended goals. We can imagine the feeling we will experience once we triumph. Once we create that feeling in our imagination, we can store it in our memories for the future. Pretty impressive, right?

Dr. Cary Middlecoff was a doctor by profession. He became a professional golfer on the PGA Tour from 1947 to 1961. "Four days before I hit my first drive in the Masters last year, I had a feeling I was sure to win that tournament," he said. In an interview for a national magazine, he said the winning feeling was the secret of winning a golf championship.

"I felt that every move I made to get to the top of my backswing put my muscles in the perfect position to hit the ball exactly as I wanted. And in putting, too, that marvelous feeling came to me.
I knew I hadn't changed my grip, and my feet were in the usual position. But something about how I felt gave me a line to the cup just as clearly as if it had been tattooed on my brain. With that feeling, all I had to do was swing the clubs and let nature
take its course."

Middlecoff said that the winning feeling is "everybody's secret of good golf, and when you have it, the ball even bounces right for you. It seems to control that elusive element called 'luck.'"

On April 13, 1997, a good-natured 21-year-old kid in a red polo shirt stunned the golf world by winning the Masters Tournament in Augusta, Georgia, with a record-breaking 18 under par. Everyone was surprised, but not Tiger Woods. He'd been visualizing that moment all his life. Earl Woods, his father, said, "He's been talking about winning the Masters since he was five years old." In his first on-camera interview, Tiger said he didn't have an acceptance speech prepared because he'd only visualized as far as the 18 hole of the final round! (Middlecoff, 1956).

SCIENTIFIC EVIDENCE AND EXPLANATION OF THE WINNING FEELING

We learn by trial and error. Every time you try something and fail, your brain records this action and stores it; the same happens when you succeed. This mechanism works based on trial and error. For example, a child is learning to tie his shoes. He watches how his parents do it and tries to repeat the actions. Every time he fails, his brain records whether his movements and actions are successful or unsuccessful.

When he finally gets it, his brain will put together all the actions or movements that led the child to succeed and store them in his memory as a success pattern. He will reinforce this pattern through practice and repetition until it is fixed in his brain. After a while, like you and me now, he can tie his shoes without thinking or even with his eyes closed.

In Psycho-Cybernetics, Dr. Maltz talks about how the science of cybernetics explains how the brain records success and failure. He provides the following explanation, given by two experts in the field of brain physiology.

> Dr. John C. Eccles and Sir Charles Sherrington tell us that the human cortex is composed of some ten billion neurons, each with numerous axons (feelers or "extension wires"), which form synapses (electrical connections) between the neurons. When we think, remember, or imagine, these neurons discharge an electrical current, which can be measured. When we learn something or experience something, a pattern of neurons forming a "chain" (or tattooing of a pattern?) is set up in brain tissue.

> This "pattern" is not like a physical "groove" or "track" but more like an "electrical track." The arrangement and electrical connections between various neurons are somewhat similar to a magnetic pattern recorded on tape. The same neuron may thus be a part of any number of separate and distinct patterns, making the human brain's

capacity to learn and remember almost limitless. These patterns, or "engrams," are stored in brain tissue for future use and then reactivated or "replayed" whenever we remember a past experience (Maltz, 1989).

Using this scientific explanation, we can see how science confirms that the brain has recorded a pattern in our brains for every successful action executed in the past. All you need to do is remember that event by replaying it in your mind. The pattern will run again, and you can now tie your shoes time after time.

What will happen if a man or woman has not ridden a bike since childhood and decides to jump on a bicycle after thirty years? They will indeed ride it again, maybe a bit unbalanced, but they will be able to ride the bike without needing to learn from scratch.

TRANSFOCREATING SUCCESS FEELING

Transfocreation is the art of taking something physical or nonphysical and transforming it with the aid of the universal laws of nature to create something new that will help you achieve a defined goal.

Let's put into practice a hypothetical situation to illustrate the concept. You feel bad because your boss decided you are no longer helpful to the company; you are laid off. Of course, you might feel bad since no one likes to be unemployed, especially if the job and the company are good for you. You are experiencing a bitter feeling as you no longer have a job. What to do next?

Let's address the emotional feeling first. The two factors, bad feelings, and unemployment, need to be addressed. One is an emotional factor, "feeling bad," while the other is physical, "not having a job." Using the law of opposites, we know that the opposite of a bad feeling is a good feeling. We can adjust the feeling since both are on the same line or scale in opposite directions.

Losing a job is not the end of the world since you are still alive and now have an opportunity to get a new job with better pay, one that is more rewarding, and a better company. This should lift your hopes and tilt the pointer toward the good-feeling side of the scale.

You realize that now you have some time off to rest, exercise, read, travel, spend more time with the family or your partner – or do things you could not do due to a lack of time. Just thinking of these opportunities will help you move the pointer toward the positive side of the scale.

We can continue looking for things to move the pointer, such as the tasteless coffee at the office for which you will no longer have to pay $2 a cup or the smelly colleague next to your work area whom you will not miss anymore. By doing this, we will move the pointer from the bad feeling toward the excellent feeling; and with that, we will thank our no longer boss for the favor he did by letting us go.

Another thing that can tilt the pointer from negative to positive feelings is the opportunity for a career change now that we are released and can explore. Now, we no longer feel bad because we were fired; we feel great due to all the positive things we gained when we switched perspectives and balanced things in a different light.

Practice makes perfect when it comes to success, feeling, and transfocreation.

Yes, humanity surges with uncontrolled passion, is tumultuous with ungoverned grief and is blown about by anxiety and doubt. Only the wise man, only he whose thoughts are controlled and purified, makes the winds and the storms of the soul obey him.
James Allen

CHAPTER 10

From Bitter to Sweet

Some people like sweet foods, others like salty, and few prefer bitter. We can all agree that there are better options than bitter food. Just by mentioning or thinking of the word bitter, it can bring to memory (licking a green lime) a taste of a bitter food or drink we once tasted in the past. We can even remember the moment we wanted to spit it out.

In this chapter, we will experience bitter and sweet, not from a gastronomic point of view but from an emotional and physical perspective. We will explore emotions and feelings that make us upset, or in other words, tense, agitated, angry, stressed, depressed, anxious, and bipolar. The ones that turn our hearts ice cold and hard as a stone. In other words, those experiences in life make us inhuman and what most people call crazy. This can happen voluntarily and consciously or involuntarily at the subconscious level without our express consent.

Whether we turn bitter because we wanted to or it just happened without our consent, we can agree that everyone notices when someone is upset, and it's not nice to be around a person in that state. A bitter person is usually negative, and we all know what negativity brings.

So, how can we turn bitterness into its opposite: sweetness? How can we become human again and recover our warm and fleshy hearts? It's easier than you could ever imagine.

Have you ever seen a baby between four months and three years crying out loud in a crib, but when the mother comes and holds the baby in her arms, the baby usually become quiet and relaxed? Why does this happen? What makes the mother so powerful is that by holding and rocking the baby in her arms, the baby transforms from a little monster kicking and hollering to a peaceful and adorable angel. The secret to human bitterness can be found and explained in this phenomenon.

By the way, it's not an outrageous and crazy idea, but that's not the point. I'm not implying that when we are bitter, angry, or sad, all we need is our father, mother, or a loved one to come over and rock us in their arms, transforming our bitterness into sweetness. We need to comprehend the source behind the mother's action and the baby's reaction.

Professor and Dr. Clancy McKenzie, M.D., founder of the Alternative Psychiatric Association, asserts that severe mental diseases are not biologically caused but have to do with delayed post-traumatic stress disorders caused by infant and early childhood separation, with onset occurring years later, starting in adolescence.

The following paragraphs from Dr. McKenzie explain the phenomena of the Unification Theory of Mental Illness.

> Everyone understands post-traumatic stress disorder caused by combat. A car backfires next to a combat veteran, and he grabs a gun and hides in the woods for a few days. His reality and behavior change to that of wartime; even his body chemistry and physiology

match that of the earlier time when his life was in extreme danger.

We 'understand' because the earlier events associated with loud noise were so life-threatening that they were indelibly etched upon his mind and brain. We fail to recognize that separation from the mother to an infant is more terrifying than war trauma to a soldier. To all mammalian infants, separation from their mother has meant death for as long as they have populated the earth. Thus, the human infant is highly susceptible to what it considers a threat of separation.

Dr. McKenzie is also opposed to SSRI anti-depressant medications, which he contends increase the chance of violence and suicide. He maintains that anti-psychotic medication shortens longevity by 25 years on average. According to Dr. McKenzie, different mental disease symptoms or episodes are a flashback to infant reality. It's perfectly appropriate behavior for an infant. We learn to do it as infants when our mother is distraught, traumatized, and distracted. It's triggered in later life by an "adult separation trauma," whether real, perceived, or anticipated. It is likely a relationship breakup, retirement, marriage breakdown, job loss, death, move, graduation, interpersonal fight, or anything that increases separation panic.

Schizophrenia correlates with early trauma because delayed post-traumatic stress disorder cannot occur without an earlier trauma. It entails a delayed post-traumatic stress disorder mechanism. People continue to have flashbacks, nightmares, and intrusive thoughts that accumulate in the age-of-origin-specific mind and brain. With each flashback, suffering, and intrusive thought, enormous repression occurs. If the trauma occurs at age one, it becomes a growing abscess of troubled thoughts in that one-year-old mind.

This serves as the wall of the abscess, which protects the individual from the painful thoughts within. As this abscess of the mind grows, the defensive wall thickens. Eventually, 10, 20, or 30 years later, there is a symptom-precipitating trauma sufficiently intense and similar to the original symptom-defining trauma that it breaks through the defensive wall, stirs this abscess of the mind and causes a volcanic eruption, and the surfacing of the unconscious material that had been repressed over the years.

Dr. McKenzie noted that thousands of events could cause the infant to feel threatened with separation and overwhelmed, and most are not apparent to the adult. This is no one's fault, and the events are unintentional. Many years later, a spouse, friend, or group rejects or leaves the person. Suppose this experience is sufficiently intense and similar to the first. In that case, the individual can flash back to the original trauma and exhibit the infant's reality, behavior, and feelings. The person also shifts brain activity to earlier developmental regions, which results in biological change (Owen Parachute, 2022).

Below is a list of the age of origin of infant separation traumas and possible disorders when triggered.

0 to 18 months - various schizophrenias

19 to 21 months - schizoaffective disorders

22 months – the peak of bipolar disorder, hypomania

21 to 24 months - psychotic depression

25 to 34 months - non-psychotic depression

After reading and analyzing this theory and explanation, you might be starting to track some of your present or past infant behavior or the one of a family member or friend to comprehend or put this theory to the test. I can't blame you because I did it myself, and it's surprising to see some accurate correlations of disorders expressed as infant behaviors in adults triggered by traumatic events.

I hope that this information and the related studies help you understand why we can become bitter and how easy it is to turn bitterness into sweetness. With awareness and understanding of the cause, we can all strive to deal with anger and other disorders we face or encounter in our families, friends, and society. By doing so, we help better our world and humanity.

*"When you see someone putting themselves out there, particularly
when you see someone is failing and failing so passionately, it brings
up this bittersweet connection to our mortality."*
Simon Helberg

CHAPTER 11

Imavizuation

The power to create is inside you. This is nothing new because you already know it. The question to ask is, what are you constructing daily? Are you building the life and circumstances you want, or are you living a life randomly determined by chance or external circumstances out of your control?

Most people, approximately 95%, live a life defined, pre-established, and controlled by others. What they live and do is what they conceive as reality. Systems, traditions, education, politics, genetic pre-disposition, and external environment influence behavior and existence.

Consider a simple rule, such as eating three times a day in the form of breakfast, lunch, and dinner, and remember that breakfast is the most important meal of the day. Who and when was that created? Have you ever stopped to investigate or (Google) it? Do you agree that most people eat three times a day? Is that the healthiest way of eating for the body and mind?

Have you ever heard about intermittent fasting 18:6 (eating in a six-hour window and fasting for 18 hours) and its benefits, such as weight control (burning fat by "ketosis"), longevity, diabetes control, and the production of growth hormone? By the way, ketosis occurs when your body burns ketones and fat for fuel instead of glucose.

It is entirely normal for the body to be in ketosis. When your body is fat-burning, it makes lots of ketones; hence, you are "in ketosis." It was a common experience for humans throughout history who had intermittent access to food and thus periods of fasting.

It's time to wake up and realize that most of the things you know or have learned from the so-called experts, education system, and cultural traditions are based on either ignorance or a lack of understanding. They are detailed and intentional decisions from entities such as Big Pharma and other federal agencies in charge of food consumption and administration.

The benefit of having "humans" sick, overweight, and addicted to drugs that might help alleviate a problem but create ten new ones is that it makes for a very profitable business. If you don't believe me, look at the side effects of any medication stored in your bathroom cabinet at home.

Enough ranting for now. It's always good to question and not take everything as accurate or at face value just because it has been presented. Being critical and open-minded might break and win the battle in your mind and leave a better world for generations.

Going back to the theme of this chapter, "imavizuation," we come to know that it's the ability to purposely create a reality in your mind and play it constantly in your mental movie theater until it comes into the flesh, or in other words, materializes in a physical form.

It is as simple as that: you now have the *"formula"* used by the greatest minds this world has ever seen for the most significant inventions and discoveries ever created and discovered. By the way, you and everyone, including me, have used this formula voluntarily or involuntarily at once. My purpose is for you to be aware of this superpower, learn how to develop and use it to accomplish your goals in this plane of existence, and when your time is up, move on to the next level and leave a better world for others.

Honestly, I don't know if the term "imavizuation" exists or has been used in the past. I tend to make up words by combining two or three words or concepts. Of course, you have already noticed this because you are reading *"The Power of Transfocreation."*

> *"If the Universe is Mental in its nature, then Mental Transmutation must be the art of CHANGING THE CONDITIONS OF THE UNIVERSE along the lines of Matter, Force, and mind. So you see, therefore, that Mental Transmutation is really the "Magic" of which the ancient; writers had so much to say in their mystical works, and about which they gave so few practical instructions. If All be Mental, then the art which enables one to transmute mental conditions must render the Master the controller of material conditions as well as those ordinarily called (mental)."*
> The Kybalion

Diving deeper into this concept reveals nothing new since the greatest and most ancient civilizations, such as the Egyptians, have mastered it to create marvels that, to this day, scientists, architects, doctors, and even the most advanced technology are still unable to explain with certainty.

A supreme and intelligent being created us. Call it whatever you want: Energy, Higher Consciousness, Brahma, Allah, Buddha, Yahweh, or God. Of course, this is for people who believe in a creator since, for evolutionists, atheists, and agnostics, the concept does not apply.

We share a common spiritual DNA with our creator. We share his likeness, which gives us the faculty to create in a lesser way than He does. A son or daughter can only have the likeness or image of their father or mother if they share the same DNA.

> *"Then God said, "Let us make man in our image, after our likeness. And let them have dominion over the fish of the sea and over the birds of the heavens and over the livestock and over all the earth and over every creeping thing that creeps on the earth."*
> Genesis 1:26 (KJV).

Tapping into our spiritual likeness or having the habit of meditation/prayer/ relaxation, we can connect and be one with the universal creative force of nature. By doing this, we can act on a plane of limitless and timelessness, where everything is possible according to our purposes, needs, and wants.

Knowing and understanding this concept can liberate you from life's ordinary and sometimes nonsense routine. It can free you from existential questioning of the why, what, and where of this tumultuous world we live in. In other words, your purpose in the bigger picture of existence.

ALTERNATE REALITIES

Quantum mechanics is a fundamental physics theory that describes nature's physical properties at the scale of atoms and subatomic particles. It is the foundation of all quantum physics, including quantum chemistry, field theory, technology, and information science.

The many-worlds interpretation (MWI) as an interpretation of quantum mechanics asserts that the universal wave function is objectively real, and there is no wave function collapse. This implies that all possible outcomes of quantum measurements are physically realized in some "world" or universe.

Quantum mechanics and physics develop different theories to explain parallel universes or the multiverse in which we live, but we are experiencing a different reality than our present one. According to this theory, you could be a rock star, scientist, politician, writer, elementary school teacher, or billionaire, and all this could happen simultaneously but in different realities.

Every major decision you make can create a different or alternate reality that will influence your future and outcome in life. Have you ever paused to think about what would have happened if you decided to skip college and start your own business after high school, or how your life would be if you moved from your country and relocated to a different country where they speak another language? What if instead of getting married, you decided to live a single life, or instead of going to school and getting a degree, you chose to become a musician and live as an artist?

Let's use a hypothetical example. You were born and raised in New York. You always wanted to become a medical doctor, so you enrolled at Columbia University after high school. You graduate and become a successful doctor, get married, live in a great apartment in Manhattan, and have two kids. That's a great story or version of a range of possibilities.

Let's assume that instead of staying in NY, you move to California and enroll at UCLA. You fall in love with an overseas student from Germany, and upon graduation, you decide to move there and start a life in Berlin. Let's make things even more interesting: you become an opera singer. After finishing high school, you enroll at the Manhattan School of Music and become an international opera singer traveling the world doing concerts.

There are infinite possibilities of future realities, all of which begin with making a decision. Because we don't know the exact outcome of our choices, we can only assume an outcome based on other people who have made a similar decision in the past, imagining a possible outcome.

Multiple possibilities and life outcomes are rooted in certain causal events. They can be big decisions such as a marriage partner or as simple as going out to dinner at a restaurant rather than staying home and enjoying a nice homemade meal.

Theories are fun and exciting to study and research or use during an interesting conversation with a friend while drinking a coffee or a cold beer. My intention is not to educate you, influence your beliefs, or spark your curiosity since I'm not a scientist or a physicist; instead, please think about the arbitrary decisions and choices we make every day and how they can alter our destinies forever.

An awareness and understanding of *"imavizuation"* will offer possible use in attaining a better outcome for our decisions. We can create and experience the desired result before physically manifesting it. In other words, decide what type of dream you want to have before you dream it, then dream it and finally make the dream a reality in physical form with the process of manifestation and materialization.

WHAT DO YOU WANT? WHAT DO YOU WANT? WHAT DO YOU REALLY WANT?

Most people never achieve anything in life because of one simple fact. They don't know what they want. Most will tell you that they want a new house, a better job, a new car, a partner, travel, or own a business. But have they ever stopped wondering and put pen to paper to describe how that house will look like: how many bedrooms, bathrooms, a front yard, a back yard, the measurements, the floor material, the cost, the neighborhood - city, state, country. What brand of car, color, price, size, interior decoration, etc.?

Would your partner be emotional? Would they help with the house duties? Will that person like to have a small or big family, live overseas, be sexually active or passive, physically fit or not? Where do you want to travel? In your same province or state, to a different country or continent, staying at a hotel or Airbnb for one week or month, maybe as a backpacker in a hostel. Own your business, yes, that's great, but doing what? A small or big company, national or international, private or publicly owned?

What do you really want? That's the most vital question to answer to begin the creative machinery. Without knowing in detail what you want, the chances of getting it are very slim because you will get a random or generic version (which you might not know until you get what you don't want); but at this point, it might be too late to reverse your outcome. This is where most people experience regrets, depression, anxiety, and unpleasant feelings over what they do, their surroundings, and life in general.

Now you can see how choices determine your future. You can look at your present life - whether good, regular, or bad - as a consequence of your decisions. It's time you owned it and accepted that while your parents, the environment, and bad breaks seem to be the cause of things you wish had never happened or would like to change, you can recreate your life. You have the ability and the right to take back control and elevate yourself above what you thought was your only option. *Transfocreate* your present and future life today.

Imagine + Visualize + Action = Your Goal

CHAPTER 12

Reverse Engineering

Reverse engineering, sometimes called back engineering, is a process in which software, machines, aircraft, architectural structures, and other products are deconstructed to extract design information. Often, reverse engineering involves deconstructing the individual components of more oversized products. The reverse engineering process enables you to determine how a part was designed so you can recreate it. Companies often use this approach when purchasing a replacement part from an original equipment manufacturer (OEM).

The reverse engineering process is named as such because it involves working backward through the actual design process. However, you often need more knowledge about the engineering methods of creating the product. Therefore, the challenge is to gain a working knowledge of the original design by disassembling the product piece by piece or layer by layer.

Humans are not machines, systems, or architectural structures. It might sound strange to consider reverse engineering in a personal development book. How can we disassemble a person, analyze its parts to see how they function, improve these parts or processes, and put it all together again? Let's open our minds for a moment. Permit yourself to see a different perspective.

The good thing about applying the concept of reverse engineering to humans is that we don't need to cut them in pieces to see how each part works because science, technology, and a thousand years of discovery and experimentation have already gathered enough information that explains how each part of our human machinery, its structure, and software (mind) works. But, of course, we never stop learning and discovering new things.

Our bodies may be compared to mechanical structures or a machine. If we compare a device, apparatus, or network ever built, none could compare to a human body and mind. We are on a different level; we are the world's most precise, complex, and developed machinery. The person with the lowest IQ is far more intricate than the most advanced supercomputer ever created. Our maker or architect created a marvel when he created man and woman.

I always compare a person to an automobile. Just like a car uses fuel in various forms such as gasoline, diesel, gas, and electricity to ignite and run the engine, as humans, we utilize food as fuel that energizes us and start our engines to live and carry on all our functions.

HOW MUCH FUEL DO WE NEED?

The capacity for energy, fuel, and storage, depends on the automobile type. Something familiar in cars is the fuel tank or electric storage capacity. A fuel tank has a storage capacity and equivalent performance in miles or kilometers per gallon. If your automobile has a 25-gallon tank and gives you 20 miles per gallon, you can drive 500 miles with a full tank. Knowing the fuel capacity and consumption of your automobile provides you with a precise idea of when to stop and refuel during family trips on your summer vacations.

I'm sure that if your tank meter indicates three-fourths (75%) of its capacity, you will not stop and fill the tank. Maybe you will wait until it's one-fourth (25%) or even when the fuel light pop-up on your dash, signaling that the tank will be depleted. At that point, you will be asking your navigation system for the nearest gas station.

What's your stomach food capacity in litters/gallons for liquid or grams/oz. For solid food? How many hours of energy does a full stomach provide before you must fill up the "tank"? Do you know when your tank is empty for sure? What type of fuel does your engine work best with? I'm pretty sure you know the answer to these questions, as you might know, the answers to the same ones when they pertain to your automobile. If you don't identify either case, it would be a good idea to find out, especially regarding your machinery.

Every person has a specific weight, height, body type, structure, and distinctive use of their body machinery. A professional football player and a lawyer may have the same weight and size, but their tank capacity and consumption will differ regarding output and performance in their respective fields.

A quarterback in the NFL (National Football Association) typically needs a minimum intake of 4,000 and up to 6,000 calories per day, depending upon the metabolism and stage of the season. An average male consumes between 2,000 and 3,000 calories daily, but this varies due to weight, height, age, lifestyle, and activity level.

Mark Mattson, Ph.D., a professor of neuroscience at the Johns Hopkins University School of Medicine and former chief of the Laboratory of Neurosciences at the National Institute on Aging, says, "There is no scientific basis for our current 'three meals a day plus snacks' eating pattern.

HISTORY OF EATING

For most of human history, people ate one or two meals daily. The current time-restricted eating patterns like the 16:8 or one meal-a-day diet (OMAD) mimic this ancient phenomenon. During periods without food, the body evolved to tap into fat stores for energy. Research shows this capability makes us metabolically and nutritionally flexible, therefore able to maintain a sporadic diet.

At what point in history did our eating habits change to what we are now accustomed to, the standard three meals a day in the form of breakfast, lunch, and dinner? Do you ever wonder why your whole day is centered on what and when you eat - or prepare to eat - including going to the grocery store to get what you fancy? It can turn into a waste of time and mental energy.

According to researchers and historians, after the era of the hunter-gatherers came the Neolithic or agricultural revolution about 10,000 years ago, which triggered tremendous health and social changes. Growing crops, raising livestock, and storing surpluses created a predictable food source. No longer were humans covering miles per day hunting big game or spending hours spearfishing in the local stream. Now, they could till the land, cultivate food, and eat more than ever. With greater food security, people no longer fasted from lack of access to food.

The three-meals-a-day plan started when farming became prominent. This became the eating pattern since people could store food, wake up in the morning, and eat. Previously they couldn't. Many people today associate fasting and intermittent fasting with a new or modern trend motivated by spirituality, health - or just trying to find meaning in life.

HEALTH BENEFITS OF RE-ENGINEERING OUR EATING HABITS

Many studies suggest that changing our eating habits can improve our health and reduce the speed of aging. The possible health benefits of intermittent fasting are extensive. To mention some: blood sugar stabilization, faster weight loss, lower cholesterol, reduced inflammation, longer lifespan, cure of type 1 diabetes, and prevention of type 2 diabetes.

Here is a simple explanation by a specialist on how intermittent fasting works.

> Each time we eat, the body releases insulin to help cells convert sugar (primarily glucose) from the food into usable energy. If the glucose isn't used immediately, insulin helps store the excess glucose in fat cells. But when we don't eat food for extended periods, insulin is not released, and the body then starts breaking down fat cells for energy, leading to weight loss and triggering different signal pathways to the rest of the body.

Intermittent fasting facilitates this process. Intermittent fasting (IF) means cycling through periods of abstaining from food (or drastically cutting food intake) with periods of normal eating. Fasts typically last from 12 hours to up to weeks at a time.

Some intermittent fasters flatter about the 5:2 diet, which involves eating normally for five days and consuming no food (or fewer than 500 to 600 calories) on two fasting days per week. Others limit their "feeding window," squeezing all their meals into six- or eight-hour periods and fasting for the rest of the day or night. Some people rave about the "one meal a day" (OMAD) diet, where people fast for 23 hours a day, then squeeze all their eating into a single hour."

I tell people that if they want to lose weight, intermittent fasting is the way. A plant-based diet is a way to go if you want to live a long time and be out of the hospital (Tello, 2020).

Below I share an abstract of an article found in the National Center of Biotechnology Information and the National Library of Medicine. The report, *Fasting: Molecular Mechanisms and Clinical Applications,* was written by Dr. Valter D. Longo, an Italian American biogerontologist and cell biologist known for his studies on the role of fasting and nutrient response genes on cellular protection aging, and Mark P. Mattson, Ph.D., Professor of Neuroscience at Johns Hopkins University, a former Chief of the Laboratory of Neurosciences at the National Institute on Aging.

Fasting has been practiced for millennia, but recently, studies have shed light on its role in adaptive cellular responses that reduce oxidative damage and inflammation, optimize energy metabolism, and bolster cellular protection. In lower eukaryotes, chronic fasting extends longevity in part by reprogramming metabolic and stress resistance pathways. In rodents, intermittent or periodic fasting protects against diabetes, cancers, heart disease, and neurodegeneration, while in humans, it helps reduce obesity, hypertension, asthma, and rheumatoid arthritis. Thus, fasting has the potential to delay aging and help prevent and treat diseases while minimizing the side effects caused by chronic dietary interventions." (Longo & Mattson, 2014).

CANCER AND INTERMITTENT FASTING

What about cancer and intermittent fasting? Let's see what the experts say. "There's a pretty strong scientific rationale for why intermittent fasting when getting chemo or radiation therapy may be a benefit," Mattson says. "That's started in animal studies, and intermittent fasting showed a slow tumor growth in various cancer models."
Most cancer cells cannot use ketones for their energy, Mattson explains. Ketones are produced by using fat stores instead of glucose and are triggered during intermittent fasting and other dietary approaches like the keto diet. Cancer cells use glucose almost exclusively.

The idea is if you have to have a patient when they're getting chemo or radiation, which are very harsh on cells, including your normal cells, if the person has low glucose and ketones are up, the cancer cells will be more vulnerable to being killed by the drugs or radiation. Since normal cells use ketones and intermittent fasting protects them against stress, the side effects of the treatment may be less (Longo & Mattson, 2014). If you would like to read the full article, you can visit: https://www.ncbi.nlm.nih.gov/pmc/articles/PMC3946160/

I'm not a nutrition expert, but my research and personal experience with intermittent fasting and fasting led me to believe what science has proved and is now recognizing to be accurate and practiced in some circles. Of course, this is not for everyone since people with specific medical conditions or eating disorders should consult their doctors or caretakers before adopting fasting and intermittent fasting to their diet routine.

USING A MORE EFFICIENT ENERGY SOURCE (FUEL)

What would you do if your auto mechanic one day told you that there is a different type of fuel for your automobile that costs the same as the one you use and has the advantage that when you fill your automobile tank, you could get not 500 miles per tank but 1,000 miles without having to stop at the gas station and fill-up. Also, this new fuel will clean your injection system, and the engine oil will sustain perfect pressure, making your automobile run faster and preserving your tires from friction.

Would you try it or stick to the regular fuel because you are afraid of trying new things and are comfortable since you have used it all your life, as your father and grandfather used the same power during their lifetimes? Some may try it, while others will stay with the same old traditional fuel system. Which one are you?

When applying reverse engineering to our bodies and minds, we should always have an open mind. When it comes to the mind, we can use reverse engineering a lot. By the way, our brains and minds are the less understood parts of our bodies. Scientists are still marveling at the infinite capacity of the brain and mind.

MIND RE-ENGINEERING

Because the traditional approach was to study the brain and mind as physical organs, the scientist concluded that we only use a minimum percentage of our mental capacity. Now, mind control researchers are catching up to the subconscious powers of our minds and the way we can manipulate and control present and future events by tapping into the subconscious mind.

When in a meditative state, our brain waves slow down to Alpha and Theta, where time and space have no influence. We can bend reality and create a new one, just as we can fix our current state and program ourselves to achieve our goals more electively than traditional programming and learning methods. Remote viewing and healing, increased creativity and inventions, problem-solving, stress, pain, and anxiety management are a few things we can affect by learning to tap into our mental powers.

You might have heard the quote, "the sky is the limit." Now, you should start thinking and believing that the sky is just the beginning since there are no limits to what you can achieve. You are a supreme powerful spiritual being, and spirit has no limits; the only limitations are the ones we perceive with our physical senses. This is where most people live their lives. You are different, and because of it, you must become more critical, investigate and learn new methods to increase your capacity, knowledge, understanding, and wisdom.

> *"For the protection of wisdom is like the protection of money, and the advantage of knowledge is that wisdom preserves the life of him who has it."*
> Ecclesiastes 7:12 (KJV).

CHAPTER 13

Relax Your Body and Mind

According to the World Health Organization (WHO), stress can be defined as "any type of change that causes physical, emotional or psychological strain." Stress is your body's response to anything that requires attention or action. Everyone experiences stress to some degree. However, how you respond to stress makes a big difference to your overall well-being (WHO, 2021).

Stress can affect both the brain and the rest of the body. Stress in small quantities can be good for people to boost energy and attention, but too much can overwhelm them, leading to a fight, flight, or freeze response. On most occasions, stress is a negative weight in people's lives that activates many undesirable outcomes. Learning how to manage stress is essential for our physical and mental health.

Before continuing, I would like to go back in time and review the initial factors or reasons why the stress mechanism was installed in our systems and its intended use. The fight, flight, or freeze response, acute stress response, or hyperarousal is your body's natural reaction to danger. It's a stress response that helps you react to a perceived harmful event or threat to survival, like an approaching car or roaring dog.

When this response is activated, it affects hormonal and physiological changes. When these changes occur, you can act quickly and self-protect. Our ancestors developed this ancient survival instinct thousands of years ago. The fight or flight mode is a defensive response system. When this system is activated, your heart begins to beat faster, your oxygen flow to your muscles, and your tolerance for pain increases. All these changes allow you to be physically ready to attack or flee.

BIOLOGY OF FIGHT OR FLIGHT

The physiological changes begin in a part of the brain called the amygdala, which is responsible for fear perception. The amygdala then sends a signal to the hypothalamus to arouse the autonomic nervous system (ANS) in charge of the sympathetic and parasympathetic nervous systems. These two systems are in control of activating the fight or flight (sympathetic nervous system) and the freezing (parasympathetic nervous system)

When the autonomic nervous system is activated, your body discharges cortisol and adrenaline - the stress hormones. When these hormones are released, they affect various organs and structures of the body and prepare them for an imminent threat. For instance, your breathing speeds up to provide more oxygen to your blood, your vision acuity increases, your hearing sharpens, the blood thickens, and the heart beats faster to provide more oxygen to your muscles.

All these physiological reactions are linked to a psychological trigger, usually fear. Instantly, you become afraid, and your body segregates the stress hormones to prepare you to run, fight or freeze. If, for example, you were attacked by a barking dog as a kid, it generated a trauma that, if not treated when you see and hear a barking dog later, can activate the automatic nervous system.

Sometimes, a non-threatening action triggers your response. For example, you are watching a movie and listening to a dog barking and chasing someone. This makes your body react, and your fight or flee becomes activated. You might be experiencing an overactive response, which can affect your physical and mental health in the long run. This is very common with people who have experienced a traumatic event and have developed an exaggerated stress response.

Our modern, overstimulated, fast-paced lifestyle makes us more anxious every day. The 24/7 news cycles, constant connectivity to electronic devices, social media, professional competitiveness, consumerism, global pandemics, and high expectations are turning us into a different type of human race.

DEALING WITH STRESS

We must find a way to cope with the new norms of life. We can't change or impact the outside world significantly because some things we see around us are not within our scope of action. We can only try to influence and affect our inner world. Our bodies and minds must learn to deal with a new society. We must learn to center ourselves to manage stress effectively.

Most of us might not have to face a roaring lion while hunting to provide our family with dinner or fight for territory for food with our neighbors as our ancestors had to. Because of this, it's essential to understand and control our body mechanisms, not to activate systems and release hormones destined to deal with life-threatening situations.

Suppose a colleague at work forgot to cc (carbon copy) you in an email with the invitation to the Christmas office party. In that case, it is not a valid reason to have a quick reaction and release lots of cortisol and adrenaline, making you want to beat them up as if you were in a boxing ring or a UFC octagon.

People think stress is bad for their health, but you need to see and understand the statistics and facts involved to understand it fully.

"People are disturbed not by a thing, but by their perception of a thing."
Epictetus

We all experience stress in different ways. How we approach life, the type of experiences we accumulate, and how we think about them make a difference when dealing with or coping with stress. Some of the most frequent sources of stress include money, work, the economy, family responsibilities, relationships, personal health issues, housing costs, job stability, family health problems, and personal safety.

Another factor that augmented stress levels were the global pandemic we experienced in 2020. The current consequences and losses to the economy and mental health are yet to be as significant as the ones we will have to deal with for many years to come.

I don't wish to alarm you with many numbers, figures, and facts about the devastating force stress cause in our economy, society, and health. This chapter and book aim to help you deal, manage, or cope with what life throws at you by creating awareness and then acknowledging and implementing the strategies that will bring you closer to your center or more natural self.

The effects of stress are devastating regarding the number of human lives it takes. All our organs and systems are affected directly or indirectly by stress. Some of the most common conditions attributed to stress are high blood pressure, heart disease, diabetes, depression, and anxiety, to mention a few.

You probably know someone who is dealing with these conditions. Some might be attributed to stress, but others not; in most cases, stress is the root cause if you dig deep into the condition's history and progression. If we investigate these conditions, you can read between the lines: dealing with them diminishes the quality of life, and a snowball effect is inevitable.

The best thing you can do is anticipate non-wanted conditions; if you already deal with them, make the necessary adjustments in your lifestyle to mitigate and reduce the adverse consequences or prevent fixing what is not broken at the moment. There are many ways to deal with stress; if you have visited a physiologist, personal coach, pastor, family doctor, therapist, or counselor, they most likely have provided a method to reduce stress.

Some of the best-known techniques to reduce stress range from physical activity, nutrition supplementation, self-care, a healthy diet, relaxation techniques, prayer, spending quality time with friends and family, cuddling, deep breathing, and spending time with a pet, to mention a few.

WHAT`S YOUR STRESS TRIGGER

When we talk about stress, it's crucial to determine the source or what triggers the response to activate your body into fight, flee, or freeze mode. You are the only one who can decide what happens. It might take a bit of consciousness of your surroundings and be honest with yourself regarding your feelings and emotions. Do not stop them from coming out but embrace them to determine where they come from and why they are present in your life.

If you wake up in the morning and feel sad, ask yourself why you feel sad. Maybe it's because of an unresolved issue with a family member or a loved one, or perhaps it's an issue at work with a coworker that you will have to face during the day, your bitcoins portfolio is decreasing dramatically, your car payment or rent is due, and you don't have the money to make the payments.

Many things can make you sad; knowing precisely what it is to mentally compartmentalize that specific issue from the rest of your life is essential. You want to make sure a problem in a particular area does not affect other areas of your life that you must manage with excellent proficiency.

COMPARTMENTALIZING

I met a brilliant and interesting friend from Slovenia in school. In one of our conversations, she spoke about how she manages the different aspects of her life by imagining other boxes or rooms in her head, each with a big label. For example, she would have one for family, school, work, friends, vacations, relations, entertainment, sports, etc.

She explained how she imagined herself entering that room or box with the label "school" when she was at school. Once there, she will only focus on school issues, not others, since she was inside the school box. That simple mental technique helped her isolate problems and prevent them from interfering with others. This was how she could perform in a more productive and focused manner.

Because I like to try new things, I immediately adopted that technique. I was in my last year of college as a student-athlete with a basketball scholarship in Kentucky. As a student-athlete, you spend lots of time practicing or playing games on the road. You miss many classes, and therefore, you don't get the opportunity to ask questions to your professors or listen to explanations that could help you understand the class subject better.

On the other side of the coin, when you are in practice or during a game, you must be 100% tuned in. You can't be there and at the same time worry about your family, friends, grades, budget, or anything else. Your mind, body, and soul must be fully present to perform at a high level. I created various boxes or rooms with labels for basketball, school, family, entertainment, relaxation time, and work (I was working part-time as a waiter in a local restaurant).

I decided to use that simple technique or mental trick when going to a basketball practice or game. I would enter my basketball compartment or box by mentally visualizing myself in front of a door or cabinet. I read the label basketball and entered through the door. Thus, I could isolate myself from other influences or issues, including school, family, money, work, and life. I was in another dimension: the basketball dimension.

When the practice or game was finished, I would see myself getting out of that compartment and back into another one, maybe a relaxation area. You can try this technique in any area of your life. It's simple to create and apply; it might help you isolate different life situations, so they don't interfere with one another.

BODY AND MIND RELAXATION

Stress is part of our daily life, and we must learn to manage it effectively. You might have tried different techniques to reduce stress. I'm sure you realize there is no single technique or method to eliminate all forms of stress. For different stressful situations, the same approach might not work. It's essential to be open-minded when learning new techniques that can be implemented quickly and easily.

There is a fascinating and effective method for relaxation and centering the body and mind. It was invented in the early 1940s and became popular in the 1960s. It then stretched around the world in the following years. It's called *The Silva Mind Control Method*. The name comes from the creator of the method, Jose Silva.

You can learn more about him and his method on his website.
https://josesilva.net/

THE WORKINGS OF YOUR BRAIN

This is how Jose Silva explains the workings of the brain and its waves:

> Your brain operates on a small amount of electricity like other computers. It can process and store information, retrieve it, and use it to make decisions and solve problems (Silva, 2022).

Unlike other computers, the electricity the brain generates for it to function does not remain at a fixed frequency. Sometimes, this electric current vibrates rapidly at 20 times per second or more. Other times, it oscillates very slowly, one time per second or less. Scientists call these vibrations "cycles" or "Hertz." They have divided the brain frequency spectrum into four segments based on the number of cycles per second, abbreviated CPS (cycles per second).

Beta is above fourteen cps, typically twenty cycles per second, when your body and mind are active, and you focus your eyes. Alpha is associated with light sleep and dreaming from seven to fourteen cps.
Theta, from four to seven cps, is associated with deeper sleep and with the use of hypnosis for such things as painless surgery. Delta, below four cps, is associated with the deepest sleep.

Jose Silva reasoned that the best range to use for mental activity would be the one with the most negligible impedance and the most energy. The alpha frequency is the strongest current-wise and the most rhythmic of the four. That is why it was the first to be discovered by scientists with their primitive sensing equipment and was named "alpha" for the first letter in the Greek alphabet."

FUNCTIONING AT ALPHA

Anything you want to accomplish in life must first be executed at the mental level and then materialize at the physical plane of existence. The exciting aspect of learning to function at the alpha level is the ability to relax your mind and body. Also, it effectively reduces stress and improves your immune system.

The most successful people on the planet can navigate or be at alpha during the day or without consciously getting to that level. These people represent 10% or less of the world's population.

They have the capacity and genius to accomplish huge goals and do amazing things. We tend to admire and be in awe of their accomplishments, thinking they are unique and made of a different genetic material than the ordinary mortal.

Let me tell you that this thinking needs to be corrected. You and I are built the same way with the same genetic material and capacity to be, have, and do amazing things. The difference relies on how we perceive ourselves and our understanding of how the spirit, mind, and bodywork. By learning to function at alpha, we open ourselves to new possibilities that would not be available otherwise.

TOXIC INTERACTIONS

We all know about or have heard of toxic relations - the ones that kill passions and destroy families, work relations, friendships, and our health in general. Sometimes, we can distance ourselves from toxic people or relationships, but now and then, they filter through the cracks of our good nature and invade us by depositing their poison in our lives.

Humans unconsciously transmit positive and negative energy to our surroundings; if it is harmful or toxic, it can affect our mood, health, and relationships. The ability to gain the awareness that these short interactions can poison our days, life and health is vital to protect ourselves. We should be prepared and protected to avoid toxicity.

By being aware of this fact, you can distance yourself from toxicity, and by repeating phrases such as: *"Negative thoughts, suggestions or images have no influence on me at any level of the mind,"* you will be able to prevent or minimize the damage. It might look simple but short self-talk can work wonders.

*"The greatest discovery you'll ever make is
the potential of your own mind."* Jose Silva

Transfogenesis

When we think about the universe, our galaxy, our solar system, and our world, it's inevitable to be amazed at how everything works like magic. Vast masses of matter are floating into space, orbiting each other with precise synchrony that can outperform the best musical symphony. All this magnificent, coordinated perfection is studied and explained by the natural science of physics, which happens to be the fundamental science.

Physics is one of the oldest academic disciplines. Over much of the past two thousand years, physics, chemistry, biology, and certain divisions of mathematics were a part of natural philosophy. Still, during the Scientific Revolution in the 17th century, these natural sciences emerged as unique research endeavors in their own right.

A multitude of invisible things could not be explained in the past by physics or science. Many alternative treatments for healing and improving health, such as acupuncture, homeopathy, and chiropractic, were not accepted as valid treatments by medical and scientific establishments. After decades of being relegated to the bin of occult arts, mysticism, or even magic, the medical establishment has accepted them as a legitimate and valid alternative for treating diseases.

ABOVE GENES

When I decided to develop the concept of transfocreation, it did not occur to me that I would begin to submerge myself in the study of our genetic composition and how genes function as programmable units of information transferred from generation to generation. This concept is called Epigenetics.

Epigenetics is the study of how your behaviors and environment can cause changes that affect the way your genes work. One of the best definitions of Epigenetics I have found to be very easy to understand is the one that the CDC (Center for Disease Control and Prevention) has on their website: "Your genes play an essential role in your health, but so do your behaviors and environment, such as what you eat and how physically active you are. Unlike genetic changes, epigenetic changes are reversible and do not change the DNA sequence, but they can change how your body reads a DNA sequence (CDC, 2022).

Our physical and mental attributes and shortcomings can be easily tracked to our parents, grandparents, and distant ancestors. We also know that our environment shapes mental, spiritual, and physical development.

For decades, science has focused on human genetic makeup as the leading cause of our evolution. With his evolution theory, Charles Darwin popularized the belief that humans evolve to adapt to the environment. With the discovery of the human genome and DNA sequencing, we can now determine what diseases a person may develop according to the composition of their genes or even choose the physical attributes we would like our kids to have, such as eye color, sex, hair color, to mention a few. Advances in science help us detect and then prevent future diseases. These discoveries could improve humankind. This last statement could be debatable depending on your principles, but it's not my job to be a moral compass for my readers.

In his best-selling book, *"The Biology of Belief,"* Bruce H. Lipton, Ph.D. confronts and debunks traditional biology and science. When he first began to share his views in the 80s on how genes are programmed by external factors (environment) – and, to be more specific our beliefs - he was ridiculed by his colleagues and the scientific community.

We all know now that his outstanding work was the basis for what we know today as epigenetics, a well-known field in science that has revolutionized our traditional understanding of the human genetic makeup.

"We live in exciting times, for science is shattering old myths and rewriting a fundamental belief of human civilization. The belief that we are frail, biochemical machines controlled by genes is giving way to an understanding that we are powerful creators of our lives and the world in which we live." (Lipton, 2016).

The Power of Transfocreation was written to help you understand that you and only you are in control of the present and future. No one is coming to your rescue. If you can read or listen to this book, I assume you are old enough to realize that past situations provoked most of our problems, limitations, and even diseases during childhood.

We don't have a known mechanism that can turn back time and redo our lives or even influence our parents and ancestors to be better programmers so we can be run by a flawless program that enables us to achieve our dreams, goals, and desires in an easy, effortless, and painless way.

From what I have learned during my experience as a human being, things are usually a bit harder than expected. But I have good news for you. Today we can transform our lives and rise to new heights beyond our wildest dreams if we learn to take control, stop blaming others, and become open to the information that can be useful on this human experience journey.

THE PROGRAM RUNNING OUR LIVES

Discoveries of the human brain tell us how most of our decisions and life outcomes are 95% controlled by the subconscious mind and only 5% by our conscious mind. How is this possible, you might be thinking? We are making decisions consciously all the time. We think of something and act on it, correct? The answer is yes, but no.

Think of it this way: imagine you are a supercomputer without a program or software. The most advanced computer is of no value if no commands or signals can be interpreted to execute a task. Let's paint a better picture: imagine a smartphone with no applications, no WhatsApp, no calendar, no weather, no call, no email, etc. Now you get the idea. Without Apps, your smartphone is useless. You might as well use it as a glass placemat.

We come into this world as a smartphone with no Apps but with the remarkable capacity to download and record many apps. The first programmers (or App stores) are our families, neighborhoods, or the culture we live in, which defines our education, religion, values, beliefs, and the perceptions we get from our environment.

The most critical Apps are given to us from 0 to 7 years of age because this is when our smartphone (brain) is very receptive to learning new things at a lower brain wave called, Theta. This allows us to record the programs we receive profoundly and fixedly.

As we get older, from 7 to 14 years of age approximately, our brains function at an Alpha brain wave level. We receive programming from our environment and life experiences, which consists of how we interpret the world, people, and life.

This programming forms the basis of our most essential and valuable Apps, which will significantly run our smartphone (life). Sometimes, the Apps programmed in us do not match the desired outcomes. Imagine that you have an App to see weather forecasts, but you need to know what time it is. That's a problem...

There are two ways to fix this issue: one will be to download an App that gives you the time or find a programmer to reprogram the weather App and make it a clock.

I hope you followed this analogy. In this example, you are the smartphone that goes to the App store and decides which ones you need. Taking it a step further, you are also the programmer who was able to reprogram the weather App into a time App to know the time.

Let's go back to the concept that 95% of our outcomes are controlled by our subconscious (App) and 5% by our conscious (we choosing the App). Remember that when we select an App (consciously), that selection only accounts for 5% of the outcomes since the way the App was programmed is invisible and runs in the background (subconscious mind). The programmer or coder already predetermined it. As stated above, family, neighborhood, education, religion, beliefs, etc. When we are kids and as we grow, we are modified by our own experiences, perceptions, education, and interactions in the world and with people, among many other variables.

I don't know about you, but I stamped on the same rock many times, fell, and hit my head, not knowing why and how this could be happening. I feel confident that I have understood the how and why of my fall. I congratulate you since you are on your way to a better life by understanding these basic concepts.

HOW TO TRANSFOCREATE AND REPROGRAM YOUR SUBCONSCIOUS

Psychologists, gurus, pastors, doctors, motivators, teachers, psychiatrists, the pharma industry, the illegal drug industry, the entertainment industry, and the alcohol industry have, in their unique way, provided a solution for the most common human mental, physical, and spiritual challenges we deal daily. We have challenges like; goal achievement, low energy, weight loss, depression, lack of motivation, suicide, mental diseases, poverty, stress, physical diseases, and low self-esteem. How to deal with all these challenges? By transfocreating your mentality.

Positive and negative thoughts have a direct effect on the way we behave. We must realize that our thoughts and behavior - positive or negative - control our biology and even reprogram our genes. Only when we synchronize our ideas with our subconscious can we reprogram our system. Then we can achieve the results we want. A happy, energized, and fulfilled life free from boundaries and limitations awaits once you learn to reprogram your subconscious mind. It's possible, and I know you will achieve it!

Your subconscious mind can be programmed in different ways. We are all being programmed and reprogrammed daily by the things we do, watch, and read. Television, the media, social media, advertisements, video games, and music are some of the most common ways. Psychologists hired by businesses create content to make people sensitive to the message intended to achieve set goals.

All this programming happens in the background without you noticing; by the time you realize it, you have already become part of a political party, bought a specific type of clothes or shoes, begun to eat a particular kind of food, and started driving a brand of car.

I see no issues with programming since it's part of life. Humans are the most unique and sophisticated machinery ever created on this planet. God created us to adapt to our environment, other people, and new circumstances.

Before successfully reprograming your system (subconscious), it is crucial to understand your current program. The way to comprehend this program is by looking at your recent results in life in different areas such as finance, love, health, social, education, professional, religion, and spirituality, to name a few. Another and the most accurate way to understand your programming is by analyzing your beliefs in all these areas. In most cases, our parents, family, and the environment we lived in during childhood served to install what is in our core and initial programs.

What do you think of money? Is it the root of evil? Do you think rich people are immoral and stingy? What are your concept of God, heaven, and hell? What happens when we die? Are you religious or spiritual? Does love make you a fool? How safe is it to love someone? Are professional people more successful and happier? What do you think of exercising and working out regularly? Are educated people better fit to live successful life? Does the future look bright or dark?

Once you have analyzed your beliefs (programs) and are confident of their effects on your life and the results they have created, you can decide if they match your desired situation and goals. If they are good due to the results you are getting, you can continually improve the program to get better results. If they are not, it's time to reprogram or delete and code a new program conducive to achieving what you are looking for.

FROM A TO I TO NEW LIFE

A. Genes are activated and programmed by our environment.

B. Beliefs represented by thoughts (positive or negative) will program your genes and results in life.

C. Your subconscious mind (program) runs and directs your life 95% and your conscious 5%.

D. Your conscious mind can program your subconscious mind.

E. Your current program is expressed by your beliefs acquired in childhood, during your life, and recent results.

F.   Reprogram your beliefs to match your desired goals and life.

G.   To reprogram your beliefs, tap into the Alpha and Theta brainwaves for your new program to stick faster and more efficiently. (Meditate)

H.   Imaginative thinking, affirmations, visualization, and repetition during Alpha and Theta brainwave activity are the most effective ways to install a new program in your subconscious.

I.   Protect yourself and your mind from programs and people not conducive to your desired goals.

Our creator's intention when he created us was for us to enjoy a happy, prosperous, and fulfilled life. He gave us all the resources in the world to possess and use for our advancement. Life is beautiful when you live it the way it is supposed to be lived.

The most profound thing he gave us is the spirituality that connects us with him. As spiritual beings, we all possess the ability to create or be creators. When I say creators, I don't just mean our capacity to invent material things, even though any material thing made was first conceived in the spiritual realm and then materialized. We can create the person we want to be during our human experience.

"The spiritual factor is what distinguishes a human being from an animal."
Jose Silva

You might have been dealt the worst cards, been born into the worst family, worst city or country, worst time in human history (a bad economy) worst environment. Not to mention bad genes! These are the cards you were dealt, but they are not the ones you should keep. You can shuffle the card deck and draw the ones you want. That's the beauty of life: nothing is fixed, and nothing is forever.

Transfocreation allows you to shuffle the card deck and get the cards you want or need to win the game of life. Taking it a step further, by utilizing *The Power of Transfocreation*, you can create a new customized deck of cards with the ones you choose.

As human beings, our greatness lies not so much in being able to remake the world—that is, the myth of the "atomic age"—but in being able to transform ourselves.
Mahatma Gandhi

FINAL WORDS

You must decide between playing the blame game or taking ownership of the wrong or right you have created or inflicted on yourself. Complaining about who, what, when, and how this or that happens will only bring on sadness, depression, and stress. When you realize that you are in control and no one is coming to the rescue, things will begin to move forward to the life you desire and deserve.

You will succeed if you want and decide to put in the work. I'm sure you are on your way just by concluding this book. Never stop searching, researching, and challenging the status quo or traditional thinking. Embrace new ways of doing things. Just because things have been done a certain way for a long time does not mean that new methods cannot give better results.

My intention in writing *"The Power of Transfocreation"* is to let you know that it's possible to get out of the hole and move from the dark to the light. It was written to give you nuggets of clarity or ideas that you can employ to improve any aspect of your life or even another person's.

Other great authors, history, personal experience, and scientific studies inspire this book's concepts.

I'm very grateful to God, my creator, guide, and source of all blessings, because, without Him, nothing is possible.

We are all one, and the One is in all of us. Transfocreate, elevate, connect, and enjoy the human experience because this life is just one stop to a long journey. Try to make it the best stop by uplifting yourself and everyone around you.

"One love, one heart, let's get together and be all right."
Bob Marley and the Wailers

REFERENCES

Leahy, S., et al. (2005). Classroom assessment: Minute by minute, day by day. Assessment to Promote Learning, 63, 19-24.

National Science Foundation (2005). A social media summarizing thought patterns. National Science Foundation.

Wattles, W. (2015). The science of getting rich: How to make money and get the life you want (1st ed.). Amazon CreateSpace.

National Geographic (2022). Your amazing brain. National Geographic. Retrieved from https://kids.nationalgeographic.com/science/article/your-amazing-brain

Hill, N. (2016). Think and grow rich (An official publication of the Napoleon Hill Foundation). (Original edition published in 1937). Sound Wisdom.

Murphy, J. (2020). The power of your subconscious mind. (1st edition). Sanage Publishing House.

Proctor, B. (2015). You were born rich. Gildan Seminars Publishers

Maltz, M. (1989). Psycho-cybernetics. (Reprint edition). Pocket Books.

Prescott, L. (1945). Self-consistency: A theory of personality. Island Press.

Dr. Hippolyte Bernheim. Archive of British Medical Journal. 1919 Sep 20;2(3064):401. PMCID: PMC2343727

Murphy, J. (2020). The power of your subconscious mind. (1st edition). Sanage Publishing House.

Maltz, M. (1989). Psycho-cybernetics. (Reprint edition). Pocket Books.

Middlecoff, C. (1956, April 1). The winning feeling. Esquire. Retrieved from https://classic.esquire.com/article/1956/4/1/the-winning-feeling

Owen Parachute (2022). Clancy McKenzie's Unification Theory Of Mental Illness: The flashback to toddler, infant separation panic. Retrieved from https://www.owenparachute.com/clancy-mckenzie.html

Longo VD, Mattson MP. Fasting: molecular mechanisms and clinical applications. Cell Metab. 2014 Feb 4;19(2):181-92. Doi: 10.1016/j.cmet.2013.12.008. Epub 2014 Jan 16. PMID: 24440038; PMCID: PMC3946160.

Tello, M. (2020, October 30). Intermittent fasting: Does a new study show downsides — or not? Harvard health publishing. Retrieved from https://www.health.harvard.edu/blog/intermittent-fasting-does-a-new-study-show-downsides-or-not-2020103021235#:~:text=By%20Monique%20Tello%2C%20MD%2C%20MPH%2C%20Contributor%20Intermittent%20fasting,that%20our%20body%20will%20use%20fat%20for%20fuel.

Silva, J. (2022). The man who unlocked the secrets of the human mind. Retrieved from https://josesilva.net/

WHO (2021, October 12). What is stress? Retrieved from https://www.who.int/news-room/questions-and-answers/item/stress

CDC (2022). What are epigenetics? Retrieved from https://www.cdc.gov/genomics/disease/epigenetics.htm

Lipton, B.H. (2016). The biology of belief: Unleashing the power of consciousness, matter & miracles. (10th-anniversary edition). Hay House.